AMERICA'S
SAILING
BOOK

by BILL ROBINSON

The Sailing Life
Bill Robinson's Book of Expert Sailing
Where the Trade Winds Blow
The Science of Sailing (*Editor*)
Legendary Yachts
The America's Cup Races (*Co-author*)
The Best from "Yachting" (*Editor*)
Better Sailing for Boys and Girls
The World of Yachting
Over the Horizon
A Berth to Bermuda
New Boat
The Right Boat for You
Great American Yacht Designers

AMERICA'S SAILING BOOK

BILL ROBINSON

Editor of *Yachting* Magazine

CHARLES SCRIBNER'S SONS — NEW YORK

Copyright © 1976 William Robinson

Library of Congress Cataloging in Publication Data
Robinson, William Wheeler, 1918-
   America's Sailing Book.
   Includes index.
   1. Sailing.   2. Sailboat racing.   I. Title.
   GV811.R57   797.1'4   76-24854   ISBN 0-684-14736-X

Contents

AMERICA'S SAILING BOOK

PART I

INTRODUCTION TO SAILING

__1

The Special Rewards and Challenges of Sailing

FOR CENTURIES, from the time man first tired of paddling his own log canoe and elevated an animal skin on a stick into the wind, sailing was the world's most important and widespread means of "assisted" transportation until in the nineteenth century, it lost out to steam-ships, railroads, and eventually automobiles and airplanes. It was a serious commercial business that no one ever thought of doing for fun.

Yet today, in the space age of supersonic speeds, with sail completely outmoded for commercial use, more people are taking to the water under sail than ever before in history. Why this paradox? Why did the sailboat fail to follow the stagecoach and the trolley car into oblivion when it was no longer a viable means of transportation?

There are many nuances to the answers to this question — nuances that will be explored, explained, and expanded upon as the subject matter of this book—but basically the answer is that sailing, an

Sailing offers an amazing range of challenges

outgrowth of a dead method of transportation, is as a form of recreation a satisfying, many-faceted way of life, deeply challenging, deeply involving, and deeply rewarding.

Despite the serious nature of seafaring as a profession and the rugged realities of life at sea, there was a glamour and romance to sail that refused to die as its commercial importance waned. An attempt to capture these qualities, to keep them alive, brought about an upswing in recreational sailing in a rise that was a direct counterbalance to the commercial decline. And strangely, the switch to recreational sailing brought about the changes in techniques and equipment that were a radical departure from eons of status quo. Professional seamen had been content to follow in the traditions and methods of generations of predecessors, and an ancient Phoenician would not have been baffled if some time machine had transported him to one of the caravels of Columbus, or even to Nelson's ships at Trafalgar. He would have recognized most of the gear and would have known what it was for and how to handle it.

Imagine the problem, though, if the time machine had slipped him but a few decades later into the engine room of an ocean liner. Even more strangely, and sticking to sail, he would be really at a loss today on the deck of an America's Cup 12-Meter, or even on a conventional ocean-going auxiliary or a racing one-design. And so, for that matter, would Columbus and Lord Nelson.

Sailing has become a sport of multiple facets, of vast variety and scope in gear and equipment, and its appeals are multiple, too. Ranging from the relaxed delight of an escapist drifting in a quiet bywater, feet on gunwale and beer in hand, to the competitive zeal of the muscular, hard-nosed crew of an America's Cup yacht, sailing offers an amazing range of challenges and rewards of contrasting philosophies and depth of involvement. No other sport called by one generic term has more subcategories and variations, and that is its true fascination. There is something for everyone—everyone who wants to can become a sailor of some sort. There are no limitations of age, sex, size, or physical prowess, except for the very young and very old who are unable to care for themselves in routine living.

Some sailors are filled with competitive zeal

What would you like to do? Would you like to be an Olympic champion, or at least one of the better sailors in your local club? Would you like to circumnavigate the globe single-handed? Would you like to win the Bermuda Race? Or would you like to get away from the pressures of modern civilization and be at one with nature and the many moods it transmits to the world of water? How about a Bahamas cruise, a trip down the intracoastal waterway, or a trade-wind passage from the Canaries to Grenada? Or maybe just a quietly pleasant sail of an afternoon on the waters of home, a change of pace, a chance to see the sun glint off dancing whitecaps and to find an isolated cove and anchor for an interlude of peace?

Sailing is a constant involvement with nature's challenge

All these and more are possible to recreational sailors. All are a part of the world they enter by becoming sailing enthusiasts, and if they are dedicated enough, they just might do every one of the above, or at least to be close to a part of each sphere of action. No one facet of sailing is self-contained, exclusive, and limiting. A sailor can be one thing one day and another the next, in a complete change of philosophy and approach.

As an example, I can't personally claim achievement in every one of the above categories, but I have experienced most of them at one time or another, and the rewards, different as they may be, can be great. I have not won an Olympic title, or come close, but I have sailed in national championships against those who have, and I have won regattas; I have not circumnavigated the globe single-handed, but I have sailed alone through far-off waters and known the peculiar challenges of a single-handed passage; I have been on prize-winning ocean racers; I have cruised in most of the prime cruising areas from Fiji to the Fyn Archipelago, from the Greek Islands to Grenada, from the Bahamas to Baja California, from Penobscot Bay to Puget Sound, and from the Virgins to the Vineyard; and yet perhaps the

A chance to poke into an isolated cove and anchor in peace

happiest hours of all have been the quiet afternoons or moonlit evenings of poking around the unremarkable two-by-three miles of channels and tidal flats that are the waters of home. In the very familiarity there is a special sense of the rightness of belonging.

At times I like competition, and sailing has given me as much of it as I've wanted: the tense muscles, the dry mouth, the split-second decisions, the intense concentration, the thrill of winning, and the dejection of defeat. At other times, I have only wanted peace and solitude and complete release from the tensions of modern living, and these too have been easy to find in a sailboat. I have come to know my family better through sailing than in any other single way, I have made some of the best and most easily resumed friendships through sailing, and I have seen many of the world's most beautiful and fascinating places from the deck of a sailboat.

I have also spent a lot of money on sailboats; have been cold, wet, lonely, and bored on sailboats; have been seasick on sailboats; and have been scared on sailboats; but none of these prevented me from coming back at the next opportunity, and in their own way, they have been challenges that have brought some of the greatest rewards. In dealing with nature, as one always is while sailing, the variations and vagaries must be met, lived with, and mastered, and this is one of the true secrets of the hold sailing has on those who are truly devoted to it. It is a constant involvement with nature, with its contrary beauty, dangerous power, and perpetual challenge. No one who has experienced this ever forgets the satisfaction and the great sense of accomplishment, renewed through each and every day of sailing.

2

The Beginnings

WHILE THE history of sail as a means of transportation and military power is older than recorded time, the story of sailing as a recreation is much shorter. It begins seriously in the early nineteenth century, but it wasn't until well into the twentieth century that sailing became a truly popular and widespread activity. In the later stages of the twentieth century, it has become the fastest-growing form of pleasure boating, and its horizons are limitless.

For centuries, the serious pursuit of commercial gain and military advantage was the whole story. There could have been occasional dreamers who went out on the water simply because it was a nice day, but they were not organized or established as a type. Some hairy aborigine might have rigged his animal-skin sail and gone out for a spin just because he liked the way the breeze was riffling across the water, but he probably didn't tell anyone what he was doing, and he no doubt caught a fish or picked a few mussels to salve his conscience. Perhaps Vikings took their long ships, loaded with a party of blonde maidens, to an island for an ox roast between raids on other settlements. Who knows? But there was no broad concept of using the sea for recreation.

We do know that Cleopatra had her barge on the Nile, and it was royalty that first frankly used boats, necessarily sailboats with slaves at the oars, for the pursuit of sheer pleasure. In England, Queen Elizabeth I used for pleasure excursions a small sailboat that went by the odd name of *Rat of Wight*, and later royalty followed her example.

It was in Holland, however, that sailboats were first used in formally organized recreation. In that maritime land, laced with every form of waterway, boats were essential for family transportation, like the family car today. As far back as the sixteenth century, there was a tradition of using these smart little sailers for pleasure outings, sort of early-day "rallies," as well as serious transportation. They were called *Jachten*, or *Jaghten*, from the word for "hunting" or "hunter" (*Jäger* in German), with a subsidiary implication of speed, hence the source of the term *yachting*. They held mock sea battles as a form of sport and social recreation.

When Charles II was called to the English throne in 1660 from exile in Holland, he started his journey in a handsome *Jacht*, with which he was much taken. As a result, the Dutch sent him a fifty-two-foot *Jacht* as a gift and, named *Mary*, it introduced the concept of *jachting*, soon spelled phonetically in English, to the world outside the canals of Holland. Since *Mary*'s one-masted rig was called *Sloepe* in Dutch, another term was transferred to English. In fact, the language of sailing is a mixture of influences from many nautical nations.

The British court and its circle developed yachting as a way of life and actually introduced racing, something the Dutch had never thought of in their rendezvous activities. Samuel Pepys became the first yachting writer of record when he described a race on the Thames Estuary between the yachts of Charles II and his brother, the Duke of York.

The sport was so royal in its ambience that there was no need for forming a club: the members of the court circle *were* a club, a highly exclusive one. It was up to the Irish in Cork in 1720 to come up with the first concept of a club for privately owned pleasure boats. Like the Dutch, they concentrated on parades, formation maneuvers, and mock battles, organized by the Water Club, and there is a line of descent, rather wavery at times, from this institution to today's Royal Cork YC, making it the world's oldest.

With Britain's seafaring traditions at their height in the era of Lord Nelson, as the eighteenth century gave way to the nineteenth, gentlemen of leisure became more interested in yachting as a means of passing the time and building their egos. A club was formed in London in 1775 to which the present Royal Thames YC traces its ancestry. In 1815, the words *yacht* and *club* were joined together for the first time with the formation of an organization called simply that: The Yacht Club, at Cowes on the Isle of Wight. Although it was primarily an organization for genteel socializing aboard yachts— which had to be at least ten tons to qualify an owner for membership—there was a match race on August 23 of the club's first summer. Most races were arranged by wagers between owners, and the crews were almost entirely professional.

Although this was a club for gentlemen, not the court, royalty had to get into the act. In 1817, the Prince Regent graciously informed the club that he wished to become a member, and eventually he asked that the club be known as the Royal Yacht Squadron. This stamp of royal privilege, placed on the sport in its early days of organization, has had a profound effect over the years. Even without royalty, clubs around the world have continued to use uniforms for officers, and burgees and flag etiquette owe much of their background and usage to this early influence, where royal standards and house colors were much a symbol of rank and power.

To its members, one of the most important perquisites of the RYS is that it is the only club allowed to use the white ensign of royalty on its yachts.

More important to the development of sailing than the fussing over ensigns and royal standards was the establishment by RYS in 1824 of a race around the Isle of Wight. There were only two boats in the race, but for the first time, a handicap was given one boat, rather than using straight boat-for-boat racing, and two important precedents were set: the establishment of traditional courses for races, and the use of handicaps for boats of different size and design. Two years later there was another important first: the establishment of a series of races during one week, with attendant balls, parties, festivities, and fireworks displays. Thus was England's famous Cowes Week started, the progenitor of many similar ones in such far-flung spots as Kiel, Germany; Bermuda; Block Island; Larchmont, New York; Marblehead, Massachusetts; southern California; and back in the birthplace of organized *jachting,* Sneek Week in Holland.

These European beginnings of the pursuit of sailing as a recreational sport were not lost on the new and growing United States of America. The traditions of sail, from small catboats poking into the tidal creeks of Cape Cod and Barnegat Bay, to the swift privateering schooners and the gallant frigates *Constellation* and *Constitution*, were strong in America, but concentrated on the traditional pursuits of commerce and militarism. There had been little time for enjoyment of leisure in the hard struggle to establish a civilization in the wilderness and then to set up a new and independent form of government. Sailboats were the only means of communication with the outside world for many American communities, and some efficient and effective boat types were being developed that were later to influence sailing for pleasure, but it was only the isolated landowner, wealthier and more conscious of European ways than most of his neighbors, who ever used a sailboat for recreation. The tidal bays and estuaries of the Atlantic Coast from Barnegat south to the Carolinas were more conducive to this, with their more leisurely, gracious way of living than that in puritanical New England, but it was a Salem, Massachusetts, bachelor named George Crowninshield who made the first big splash in America as a recreational sailor.

"Cleopatra's Barge" was a smart sailer for all her luxury

At the age of fifty, loaded with privateering profits from the exploits of his family's vessels in the War of 1812 and bored with his desk-bound duties in shipping, he decided to go to sea—not, however, in one of the Crowninshield commercial vessels. A bon vivant and something of a dandy in dress and manner, an extrovert to make up for his stocky five-foot-six stature, George was tired of New England life and longed for warmer, more easy-going climes. His father had died, leaving him free to indulge his whims as a senior member of the family, and the result, in 1816, was a hundred-foot brig. To make clear her frivolous purpose, he named her *Cleopatra's Barge*, remembering the ornate vessel, canopied in cloth of gold, in which the Queen of the Nile had come to meet Mark Antony. She was America's first real sailing yacht.

She was built right in Salem by a shipwright named Retire Becket, whose family yard had been founded in 1655, for the then-stupendous base price of fifty thousand dollars. By the time George finished adding "optional extras" the bill was a lot higher, as she was fitted in a style of high luxury with velvet cushions, mirrors, settees, and the best in china, silver, and porcelain, with gold and bronze ornaments and many lavish touches. As a final whimsy, each side of the hull was painted in a different way. The starboard side had a horizontal pattern in contrasting colors, and a strange zigzag scheme covered the port side.

She was launched November 21 amid great pomp and ceremony, and the winter was spent in outfitting her for a junket to the Mediterranean. She might have had bizarre frivolity as her purpose, but she was a sound, fast-sailing vessel in the best tradition of the Crowninshield commercial ships. With an owner's party of George's special friends aboard, she cleared Salem March 30, 1817, with the whole town out to see her off, and made a fast passage to the Azores. From there she entered the Med and spent the spring and summer in a grand tour of its ports. Through family connections in Washington, where his brother was President Madison's Secretary of the Navy, George had entrée to top European circles, and the cruise was a round of parties, receptions, and sightseeing. The *Barge's* complement went sightseeing ashore, and curious visitors boarded the vessel in droves to gawk at her appointments, particularly at a cigar-store Indian in full regalia as a fixture on deck.

Despite a few personality clashes and the wear and tear on the ship's fittings and appointments from the constant stream of visitors, the cruise was a great success. George was planning more cruises, but a heart attack killed him a month after the voyage was over. Thus ended the first grand-style use of sailing for recreation in America, and there were no similar developments for a few years. George Crowninshield had been unique, and his style of yachting put him well ahead of his time.

While Crowninshield was whirling his friends around the Mediterranean, there were stirrings in the New York area that were eventually to lead to more lasting developments and influence on recreational sailors than the cruise of *Cleopatra's Barge*. These were along different lines: the pursuit of sailing as a competitive sport and a field for scientific development. One of the prominent families in the area was that of Colonel John Stevens, an early steamboat pioneer, whose home was a landmark of the west bank of the Hudson River, perched high on a bluff over Castle Point in Hoboken, New Jersey. Among his twelve children were inventors, educators (Edward founded Stevens Institute), and one ardent sailor, John Cox Stevens. As early as 1809, when he was twenty-four, John had a twenty-foot sailboat named *Diver* which he used for sport on the Hudson, and his interest was awakened early in the technical challenges of sailing, rather than in the chance for ostentatious luxury.

In 1816, the year *Cleopatra's Barge* was causing such a stir in Salem, Stevens built a fifty-six-foot cat-rigged schooner based on the pirogue, a type of Caribbean dugout canoe. She was named *Trouble*, and she was an early example of his continuous interest in adapting types of traditional commercial vessels to recreational sailing. His next experiment was a catamaran with the obvious name of *Double Trouble*, but she was not a success, and he went back to monohulls based on less exotic prototypes.

John Cox Stevens could be called the "father of American yachting"

His next sailboat was the sixty-two-foot schooner *Wave*, borrowing from a type of commercial vessel familiar in New York waters. Before having her built, he had tested a scale model by sailing it off Castle Point against another model. As a result of the tests, he lengthened the design by four feet, and the boat was a success in local pick-up races and also in a foray against the best that Boston could offer in 1835 and 1836. It is interesting that these tests took place right off the present location of the famed Davidson towing tank at Stevens Institute, a facility that has played such an important role in modern yacht design.

Ever curious about the mechanics of making a sailboat go faster, Stevens introduced some innovations that were far ahead of their time in his next boat, the ninety-foot *Onkahye*. Her hull form had flaring topsides and hollow garboards, and she had a thick fin keel with outside ballast. Her masts and booms were fitted with slides and sail tracks instead of the conventional parrels (hoops) and lashing, and she proved very fast in some ways but slow in stays and a wicked roller.

Back at the drawing board, he came up next with *Gimcrack*, a beamy fifty-one-foot schooner with bluff bows. She was not too successful in racing, and he did not keep her long, but she has one claim to lasting fame. It was in *Gimcrack's* saloon on July 30, 1844, at anchor off the Battery, that the New York Yacht Club was formed, the first one in the United States. The first club activity was a cruise to Newport, Rhode Island, and the club cruise in New England waters has been a tradition ever since. It wasn't until the next summer, on July 17, that the first club regatta was held, down the harbor to a buoy in Lower New York Bay and back, also starting a long tradition, and sailing as a formal sport had been launched in the United States.

Gimcrack disappointed Stevens by taking a third in this regatta, and the family rallied around to produce a faster boat.

Stevens's brother Robert, an inventor and designer, worked out the first real racing machine in sailing history, the 92-foot sloop *Maria*, with John Cox and another brother, Edward, the educator, as

A model of "Gimcrack" in whose saloon the New York YC was founded

co-owners. The design was based on the fastest local commercial boat, the Hudson River freight sloop, which had to be swift and able to negotiate the tides, currents, and tricky winds in the stretch between Albany and New York. The replica sloop *Clearwater*, built in 1969 to promote environmental awareness on the Hudson, is a modern counterpart of the type. After experimentation, *Maria* was lengthened to 110 feet, and for years she was the fastest boat in the harbor and virtually unbeatable. She had hollow spars, tracks and slides for the sails, a steering centerboard counterbalanced and supported by coiled springs, outside ballast in tapered lead strips, and a huge 12-foot tiller. Her spread of sail was 7,890 feet.

Maria was particularly good in the smooth waters of the harbor and Lower Bay, but she was too much of an overrigged machine for offshore work, and she was dismasted several times. Her speed and local success whetted Stevens's appetite for competition in more distant areas. He realized she was not the right boat for competition

"Maria" was the first real racing machine, years ahead of her time

*Some of the original models
of early racing yachts*

because of her tremendous rig and sensitive gear. The upshot was the development of the schooner *America* and her voyage to England in 1851 to take part in racing at Cowes.

That event, which will be treated more fully in the chapter on the history of the cup it won and brought home, was a milestone in recreational sailing, which it established as the first truly international sport. The event also established traditions and set influences in motion that are still very strong in the tremendous proliferation of sailing today.

Following New York's example, clubs were formed in many other areas. Southern YC, in New Orleans, came five years later, and Carolina YC, near Wilmington, was founded in 1852. The unsettled times leading to the Civil War, and the war itself, slowed the surge for a few years and only Buffalo YC (1860) and Neenah-Nodway on Wisconsin's Lake Winnebago (1861) survive today from that era. With the war out of the way, thoughts turned once again to

"America" leading the way in the 1851 race around the Isle of Wight

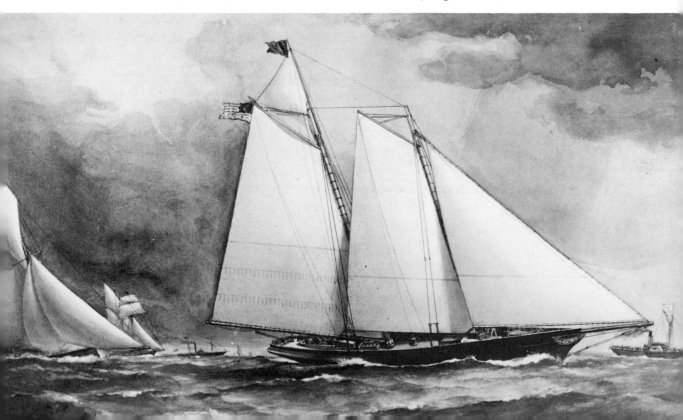

recreation, and clubs proliferated rapidly in every area, coast to coast and inland. Still important commercially despite the inroads of steam, sailing had begun the swing to a recreational activity in all earnestness.

The boats still reflected commercial influences, however. *America* had been based on the swift pilot schooners that patrolled the entrances to major ports and raced to meet incoming ships, with the winner getting the job of putting a pilot aboard. After *America's* success, most large yachts followed her example. Although they were being built as yachts, they still had the look of the pilot boats.

Some of these were luxuriously appointed as showpieces, but most sailboats were intended for racing, and the trend to ostentation and opulence in the Crowninshield tradition manifested itself mainly in steam yachts. As the base for recreational sailing broadened from the very rich to those simpler tastes and lower (but not low) incomes, smaller sailboats were converted from such commercial types as catboats, bugeyes, sharpies, oyster sloops, and many other localized varieties. The new yacht clubs began to sponsor races for them, such as the Toms River Challenge Cup for catboats on Barnegat Bay, inaugurated in 1871 as a handicap event.

Each area had its own boat types, and there was no overall organization or uniformity to the racing. Occasionally groups from one area would travel to another one to borrow boats there and engage in some intersectional competition, but the latter part of the nineteenth century was mainly an era of isolated local growth, with more and more clubs being formed and making gradually more formal attempts at organizing small-boat racing.

The renewal of America's Cup competition in 1870 with the first British challenge had a profound effect on the development of larger yachts. The first few matches were held in schooners that were essentially replicas of commercial boats, but the intensity of the competition, and the prominence the event soon achieved as a premium international sporting competition, changed all that. Before

Barnegat Bay in New Jersey, a fifteen-foot slipper-shaped boat built by J. Howard Perrine, known as a *sneakbox* from its origins as a duck-hunting boat, gained favor with many local clubs and was used for interclub racing. Over three thousand were built by Perrine over a period of about fifty years, starting in 1900.

In some areas, clubs began to band together in associations to sponsor interclub racing and standardize boats, rules, and equipment. Such an organization started on Long Island Sound in 1895, clubs around western Lake Erie formed the Inter-Lake YA in 1894, and lake clubs in the upper Midwest started the Inland Lake YA in 1897, among the early ones. The latter featured racing in *scows,* slender blunt-nosed speedsters whose devotees claim they provide the most exciting sailing there is, and they were among the earliest one-design types in organized sailing.

The first class to spread one-design racing over a wide area, and eventually internationally, was the Star Class. George A. "Pop" Corry, a veteran Port Washington, Long Island, small-boat sailor, felt there was a need for an inexpensive boat that would still provide top-level racing, and in 1911 he asked the naval architecture firm of Gardner and Company to provide a design. William Gardner had designed a small boat called the *Bug* in 1907, and Francis Sweisguth of that firm adapted the Bug design into a twenty-two-foot-seven-and-a-half-inch chine-keel sloop dubbed the *Star*. A fleet of twenty-two was built for racing that year, and another eleven were built in Nahant, Massachusetts. By 1915 there were enough Stars to form the Star Class Association with Corry as its first commodore, and he worked hard to establish the class locally, firm in his enthusiasm for a boat that could provide fine racing for sailors who did not have to be rich to own one. His successor, George Elder, widened the horizons of the class to Great South Bay, the Chesapeake, Lake Erie, New Orleans, southern California, and Chicago, and a new concept in sailboat racing was established.

The Star eventually went international and is still run by a strong

The Star (in modern dress) was the first real one-design class

group today, a model of organization for other classes, of which there were many more to follow. Local favorites like Beetle Cats in New England and Snowbirds in California helped build one-design racing regionally, and the Depression of the 1930s gave an added boost to the concept of low-cost one-design boats that would not lose their value by being quickly outbuilt. The Snipe, Penguin, Comet, and Lightning were born during the 1930s, given a great boost by the fact they could be built relatively easily by home builders, and the Star, once the poor man's boat, gradually developed into the real gold-plater of the one-design world.

With the onset of the fiberglass revolution after World War II, plus the proliferation of new man-made lakes throughout the country, on many of which powerboat use was restricted or prohibited, and the great growth in leisure-time interests, one-design sailing really took off. Hundreds of classes were established, some to wither and die

The Snipe became popular because it could be easily home-built

soon, others to grow in strength and prestige. One-design racing is now the largest and most popular organized activity in sailing. As one small example, my home club, Shrewsbury S and YC, had nine boats in 1953 and has over one hundred now.

While the twentieth century was bringing this type of growth to sailing, spreading it to a broad base financially and geographically, another quite different form of sailing was also developing: ocean racing. Perhaps inspired by the fast passage made by clipper ships on the California, China, and Australia runs, wealthy yachtsmen of the late nineteenth century occasionally had their yachts race across the Atlantic. The first such event was in 1866 when *Henrietta*, *Fleetwing*, and *Vesta* raced from New York to England in December, of all months, for a sixty-thousand-dollar wager that came out of a drinking session at a New York club. The boats were manned by professionals and only one owner was aboard. That conditions were rugged, even for hardened professional seamen, was dramatized by the loss of six men from *Fleetwing* when her cockpit was swept by a big wave. *Henrietta* won.

There were a few other races of this type, but nothing formal, and offshore racing really got its organized start in the 1898 Chicago-Mackinac Race, which also came out of a hot-stove-league argument at Chicago YC the preceding winter. At 333 miles the longest regularly run fresh-water race, it is the granddaddy of them all.

The first formally organized salt-water race was in 1905 for the Kaiser's Cup, with much attendant publicity, and the 185-foot schooner *Atlantic* won it in twelve days, four hours, one minute, and nineteen seconds, a record that still stands. The Bermuda Race was started in 1906, languished, and came back strong after World War I in 1923 to become the premier blue-water fixture, and the Honolulu Race also started in 1906. It was a hit-or-miss kind of sport, however, until the Bermuda Race began to create legends and heroes. Other events, such as the St. Pete-Havana and Miami-Nassau Races, added glamour to the sport during the 1930s, and the end of World War II saw the beginning of an unprecedented boom in it. It is the most complicated, involving, and expensive sport known to man, but its devotees pursue it with undying zest.

Another well-publicized form of sailing, long voyaging, also came into vogue around the turn of the century. The Lindbergh of the long voyagers was Captain Joshua Slocum, a retired ship captain who rebuilt a decrepit old thirty-six-foot sloop named *Spray* in Fair Haven, Massachusetts, and circumnavigated the world solo. When he arrived home in 1898, he was a world celebrity and was soon followed by many imitators, some pure publicity-seekers. The vogue for long passages under sail grew slowly until World War II and then, like every other phase of sailing, really took off in the postwar years.

In contrast to the hard-nosed competitors in one-design sailing, the money-spending masochists in offshore racing, and the peculiar breed of long voyager, whether solo or with crew, the great majority of recreational sailors go afloat mainly to relax, in either day sailers or cruising auxiliaries. The biggest numbers are in this category, and the opportunities for them to enjoy themselves are limitless. Just as the fiberglass revolution helped organized racing, so has it made the more relaxing forms of sailing easier to pursue.

In addition to the opening up of new bodies of water in areas where there had never before been any sailing, the use of fiberglass, and in some cases aluminum, created new boat types that could be used in more ways than the older, conventional planked and caulked wooden boat. No longer did boats have to stay in the water to keep them from drying out, opening their seams, and leaking. They could be *dry-sailed* out of club and marina parking lots, a much less expensive arrangement than new slips or dockage. No longer was a club or town fleet limited by the amount of dockage and mooring space in its harbor.

Dry-sailed boats could also be easily trailed behind the family car, with their seamless hulls able to stand up to the shocks and stresses of road travel. At first it was racing sailors who took advantage of this feature, trailing their boats to distant regattas and widening the scope of the sport tremendously. The racers were followed by the day-sailing crowd, who liked the idea of sampling different bodies of water, and the practice also spread to small cruising boats, big enough to sleep two or four, able enough to cruise in most of the popular areas, yet small enough to be towed by a private car.

From a log canoe under a stretched skin to today's plastic trailables, recreational sailing has come a very long way and has spread to a tremendous number of people.

___3

Rigs and Terminology

THROUGH ALL the centuries of use and development of sail-boats, there have been countless variations in the basic principle of putting a piece of cloth up on a stick to catch the wind and harness it for motive power. In all parts of the world, described in many languages, the cloth and the stick or sticks have been put up in a vast number of combinations, all for the same purpose, and these combinations are known as rigs. Out of the variations, there has been a relatively simple standardization in modern times. Most boats are one of two rigs, but there are other rigs that are also seen fairly common-ly. The two rigs that are numerically dominant in modern recrea-tional sailing are the cat rig and the sloop rig.

Single-Masted Rigs

CATBOAT The simplest rig of all, usually just called the cat rig not to be confused with the slang abbreviation for the twin-hull configuration known as the catamaran, consists of a single sail, with the mast

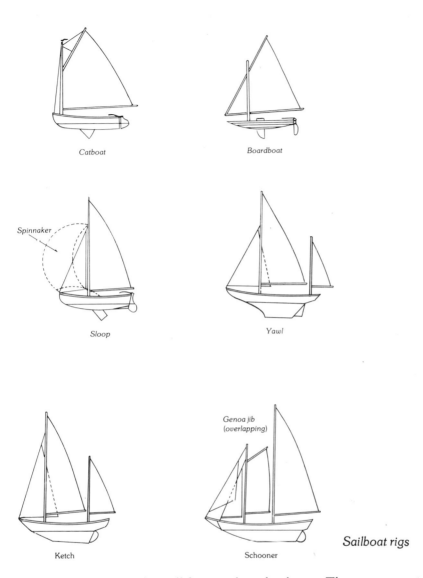

Catboat

Boardboat

Spinnaker

Sloop

Yawl

Ketch

Genoa jib
(overlapping)

Schooner

Sailboat rigs

located, or stepped, well forward in the boat. There are variations on the catboat rig, such as the triangular Marconi sail; the four-sided gaff sail; and the lateen, sprit, and gunter sails. Most small sailing dinghies are catboats, and the *Marconi rig* is the most common. It is called *Marconi* because its introduction coincided with the introduction of

A one-design sloop (the Snipe)

radio, and the taller masts needed for the triangular sail, in contrast to the conventional gaff rig, were compared to the tall masts needed for wireless radio.

The gaff-rigged sail had been the traditional one for generations, with a four-sided sail hoisted on a relatively short mast. The sail has a boom at the bottom and a gaff on its upper edge. With this arrangement, a good-sized sail area can be hoisted on a short mast, which need not have many stays to support it, compared with the taller Marconi mast which needs staying. Since a catboat mast is right up in the bow of the boat, it is difficult to get an effective staying angle, and a shorter mast is preferred. For this reason, the gaff rig has remained popular for all but the smallest cat-rigged dinghies, even though the triangular Marconi sail is a bit more efficient as an airfoil.

Gaff-rigged sails can be found in all rigs described here, but they are more common in catboats.

The lateen, gunter, and sprit rigs are basically similar. Their prime function is to provide sail area aft and forward of the mast while only using a single sail. That permits moving the mast farther aft in the boat, where it is more easily supported, and also provides a balanced rig. Most modern boardboats, the simple sailing surfboards that have become so popular, use the lateen rig to good effect.

A small boat with any of these variations of a single-sail rig is easy to handle, simple to rig, and less expensive to fit out. It is more difficult to achieve balance with a single sail, and catboats are famous for being hard on the helm. Especially off the wind, a great deal of pressure must be exerted on the helm to keep them under control. For this reason, catboats are seldom very large. There have been big ones built in the past, up into the thirty-foot range, but the rig is mainly suited for small dinghies and boats up to about twenty-two feet. Above that size, the single sail has too much area in one spread to be efficiently handled by a small crew. It is better to split up the sail area into more manageable combinations.

SLOOPS Popular as a rig with the Dutch *Jachten* as far back as the fifteenth and sixteenth centuries, it is now the most common rig for

The Olympic single-hander, the Finn, is a Marconi catboat

everything above the size of the smallest dinghies, and some of them can even carry a sloop rig. In a sloop the mast is stepped roughly a third of the way back from the bow, and the area forward of it is filled by a triangular sail, the jib. Most sloops are now Marconi-rigged on the mainsail, the larger sail aft of the mast, although occasional gaff-rigged relics can be found as in all types. With the mast located in a wider part of the boat than in a catboat, it is easier to stay it efficiently in a sloop. Higher masts are therefore more practical, and there is no need for keeping the rig low with a gaff-rigged main.

A properly designed sloop rig provides for an interplay between the jib and main that sets up a more effective flow of air over the sails than the single sail of a catboat can produce, although there are many variables, which will be discussed in Chapter 4.

CUTTERS   A cutter is a variation on the sloop rig. If you enjoy arguing, you might start a discussion of the exact definition of a cutter. There is no hard-and-fast rule that says a cutter has such-and-such a percentage of sail area in the main in relation to the jib, as compared with a sloop. An owner can decide for himself whether he has a sloop or a cutter, but in general, the mast of a cutter is located farther aft, and it very often has more than one headsail, instead of the single jib of a sloop. The term *cutter* has become a bit old-fashioned and denotes a more traditional vessel. Today most boats with a single mast and a jib forward of it are called sloops.

Divided Rigs

YAWLS   Leaving single-masted rigs, we come to divided rigs: boats with more than one mast. A yawl is a two-masted vessel, with the larger mast, or *mainmast*, forward and the smaller mast aft. This is the *mizzen,* sometimes also referred to as the *jigger*. In a yawl, the mizzen is relatively much smaller than the main, and it is stepped aft of the location of the boat's rudder post.

KETCHES   The ketch also has the mainmast forward and the

mizzen aft, but the mizzen is relatively taller than that of a yawl, and it is stepped forward of the boat's rudder post. If a boat's rudder is hung all the way aft on the transom, it has to be a ketch no matter what the relationship between the masts.

Both yawls and ketches can have gaff-rigged mains or mizzens, though this is not common any more, and they can also be cat-rigged, with the mainmast stepped all the way forward, doing away with any headsails.

SCHOONERS   The schooner is an old-fashioned rig, seldom built any more, except in replica vessels, although many older schooners have been preserved as classics. A schooner has two or more masts, with the smaller mast forward.

Square Rigs

All these rigs have fore-and-aft sails: sails whose leading edge is attached to a mast and whose neutral position is along the bow-to-stern axis of the boat. Very few modern boats have square-rigged sails of the type used on sailing vessels for centuries. The spars of square-rigged sails are attached to masts at the spar's center, and the neutral position of the sail is across the hull. Square rigs are now seen only on replica vessels and some of the "tall ship" training vessels still in existence. These are the major square-rigged types that still might be encountered:

Ship. A vessel with square rig on three or more masts.

Brig. A two-masted square-rigger

Bark (Barque). A three- (or four-) master with square rig on the forward masts and fore-and-aft on the mizzen

Brigantine. Square-rigged on the foremast and fore-and-aft rigged on the main

Barkentine. Square-rigged on the foremast and fore-and-aft on two or more masts

Brigantine (left) and schooners are now rarely seen

Sails

Within the basic fore-and-aft rigs common in sailboats today, there are many special sails, rigged under certain conditions to get the most out of the sail area possible on the masts a boat has. Most of them are for racing, though some of the sails also are helpful for day sailing and cruising.

SPINNAKERS are large, balloon-like sails for off-the-wind work. The name supposedly comes from its first use—on an English boat named *Sphinx*. It was so large, that it was known as *Sphinx' acre*, a story that can be taken for what it's worth. Modern spinnakers, made of brightly hued nylon in many combinations of stripes and patterns, add a splash of color to the sailing scene. They are flown with their sides and foot free, attached only at the head and at both corners, one to a spinnaker pole sticking out horizontally from the mast and the other to a controlling line or sheet. In sophisticated racing, spinnakers come in many different cuts and shapes for very special conditions. They give tremendous lift to boat speed but are also the trickiest sails to control, and their use is one of the advanced arts in sailing.

GENOA JIBS   The type of large jib that overlaps the mainmast and is trimmed well aft alongside the mainsail on its leeward side is known as a *Genoa jib*, or *genny*, because it was first used by a Swedish sailor named Sven Salen in a 6-Meter race in Genoa during the 1920s. On many modern boats it is the single most powerful sail, outranking the mainsail in importance, and the *slot effect* of the wind between it and the leeward side of the mainsail is a major factor in boat speed. Genoa jibs are measured and referred to by their size in relation to the foretriangle: the area formed by the mainmast, the foredeck, and the headstay of the boat. This is expressed in percentages—a 150 percent Genoa overlaps beyond the foretriangle by 50 percent of the area of the foretriangle. There are also special types of overlapping jibs for special wind conditions such as *reachers, drifters,* and *genakers.*

STAYSAILS   There are many kinds of staysails. If a boat has more than one headsail, the inner one is a staysail. Staysails, specially cut and of varying weights, can also be set in combination with spinnakers in the foretriangle, on the forward side of mizzen masts, and between the masts of schooners. Because of their great variety in shape, function, and size, they have been given nicknames such as *tall boys, bloopers, cheaters,* and *floaters.* Some of the names come into common usage; others disappear after a season or two.

SPECIAL SAILS   In addition to this array of oddball sails, schooners developed a whole set of their own special sails, such as *gollywobbler* or *fisherman's staysail,* large sails hoisted between the masts in light weather. As for the names of the sails on square-riggers, we won't go into that highly involved subject in a book on pleasure sailing.

Hull Forms

These rigs and sail variations go on a great range of hull forms. There are basic types and variations within types, depending on size and intended function.

MONOHULLS The greatest number of sailboats are monohulls, boats in which the hull is one construction unit. They can then be of displacement form, sitting in the water and pushing through it; light displacement, able to lift partially out of the water under certain conditions; or planing types that lift on top of the water and skim over it if given enough wind. Hulls can be round-bottomed, flat-bottomed, V-shaped, or modified V. Boats whose bottom and side meet at a sharp angle, known as the *chine*, are said to be *hard-chined*.

Most monohulls have a conventional pointed bow, but some are slipper-shaped, with broad, flat hulls and rounded bows, and are known as *scows*, an inelegant name for lively performers. Sailing surfboards are almost flat-bottomed, or very shallow V, and are known as *boardboats* or *sailboards*. The Sailfish was the first brand name to achieve popularity in this type, and many people refer to all makes of this generic type by this term, or that of its successor, the Sunfish.

To prevent leeway, or slippage sideways, monohulls need some form of lateral resistance underwater. Heavy-displacement boats, and some lighter types, have fixed keels with weight, known as *ballast*, on them, to prevent leeway and to help stability. If they should capsize in extreme conditions, the ballast will help them to right themselves. In lighter planing boats or small-displacement boats, lateral resistance is provided by a vertically adjusting centerboard or dagger board that slides up and down and whose depth can be controlled. Ballast in light boats must be provided by crew weight, as the boats will capsize in a breeze if weight is not properly distributed.

MULTIHULLS Boats with more than one construction unit for hulls are not as numerically popular as monohulls, but widely seen in small day sailers and racing boats, and in larger cruising models. Multihulls can achieve very high speeds in off-wind work. They skim at or near the surface with very little resistance, as their hulls are narrow and knife-like in the water. They are not generally as close-winded as monohuls in going to windward. They are very stiff and stable in normal conditions, hardly tipping at all, but they do lack ultimate stability. If capsized by a big wave or high winds, they cannot be righted again. This is a danger for offshore passaging, but many monohulls have completed transoceanic voyages and circumnavigations when carefully and correctly handled.

CATAMARANS are twin-hulled boats with hulls joined by a bridge deck. There are two types of catamarans, *symmetrical* and *asymmetrical*. In the former each half of each hull matches the other half in shape. In the latter, the hulls match each other, but the sides of each hull don't match. One is relatively straight, the other more curved, and the pressure set up by the differently shaped sides helps prevent leeway. Symmetrical hulls usually need some form of board or fin keel.

TRIMARANS are three-hulled boats, usually with a large center hull and smaller pontoon-like hulls which are attached by struts to each side.

Multihulls can be *cats, sloops, ketches,* or *yawls,* depending on size and function.

Fittings

To handle the sails and assist the rigging, a sailboat has a number of special fittings. On a maxi ocean racer they comprise an overwhelming array of hardware, while a simple dinghy or day sailer has just a few basic pieces of equipment.

CLEATS There are many shapes of cleats for making lines fast. The familiar deck cleat with a central base and prongs extending out from it performs many functions, from fastening halyards to mooring lines. Cleats should always be through-bolted, with a backing plate if positioned on thin material, never screwed in place. In racing sailboats, jam cleats are very useful for quick positioning on lines in tension without having to make the usual figure-eight loops around conventional cleats. A notched, movable, spring-tensioned part that

A mainsheet jam cleat on a small one-design, plus blocks on boom

jams against line under tension, holding the line against a fixed notched part, performs this function quickly and efficiently, and it may be freed with a flick of the wrist. Jam cleats can also be attached to blocks, such as on the mainsheet trimming assembly, for instant trimming and firming.

TURNBUCKLES   are adjustable fittings attached to the end of fixed rigging so that the tension may be changed by turning the barrel of the turnbuckle on the opposite-rotation threaded bolts that go into each end of the barrel.

STAYS   are wires for fore-and-aft bracing of a sailboat's rig. Some stays are grooved so that headsails can be raised in them.

SHROUDS   are wires for athwartships bracing of the rig. Both stays and shrouds usually have turnbuckles at their lower ends. Shrouds are attached to fittings called chain plates. *Tangs* are the fittings on the mast for attaching shrouds and stays.

SPREADERS   are braces crossing the mast to hold the shrouds out at a more efficient angle.

WINCHES   are geared, rotating drums that add power for trimming sails under heavy tension. Lines are always placed on them clockwise.

TRAVELERS   provide for athwartships adjustment of mainsail trim. They can be a *bar*, a *grooved slot*, or a *sail track*.

BLOCKS   are nautical pulleys and come in many shapes and variations, depending on function. The rotating part is called a *sheave* and the frame is the *shell.* Closed, single-sheave blocks are used for running permanent lines, such as mainsheets. *Cheek* blocks are attached to a surface and can be used for reversing the direction of a line to give it the most efficient lead. *Snatch* blocks have a shell that can be opened sideways for quick removal of the line without running it all the way through. Multiple blocks are used to gain extra power on mainsheet assemblies and other tackle where heavy loads must be handled.

SHACKLES are U-shaped fittings for attaching other fittings to each other and come in many weights, shapes, and sizes. Some have a pin that screws in place, while others are closed by spring action or flexibility under hand pressure for quick release. The pins that hold shackles and turnbuckles in place are called *clevis pins,* and these are secured in place by *cotter pins,* small double wires that fit through a hole at one end of the clevis pin and then are locked in place by splitting and spreading their two parts.

We could go on at the length of a complete catalog of marine hardware, but those are the major categories of fittings encountered on the normal sailboat.

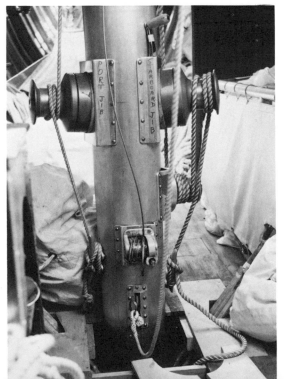

Halyard winches on a 12-Meter —important fittings

___4

How a Boat Sails

THE MECHANICS of sailing are at once simple and very complicated and sophisticated. It is easy to understand how wind blowing against a surface can transmit its power to a force on that surface that can be made to drive a shape across water, if it is thought of as merely blowing the shape directly downwind. Put a rag up on a stick attached to a shoebox and the box will be blown downwind. In some areas of the world, where the wind always blows in one direction, this is all that is needed to cross an ocean, and primitive sailboats were little more than a rag on a shoebox. When it was impossible to get where you wanted by blowing downwind, you broke out paddles or oars to proceed in other directions. Much early communication by sea depended on winds that blew steadily in one direction, and it is truly amazing that little advance was made on this principle for century after century.

Gradually it became apparent to ancient mariners that sail could be harnessed to drive a boat in a variety of directions, but understanding of how this was possible was slow in developing. Even today, the fine points of the aerodynamics of sailing are subject to experimentation and further study. If sail were as important to man as the jet plane, or as advanced-seeming as a rocket to the moon, research and development would no doubt be of an extremely high order. Since the major use of sail is now recreational, it is only the pressures of competition, the urge to win, that produces new studies and new developments in how to make sail power more efficient. That involves the shape, texture, weight, support, and trim of the sailcloth, and the shape, weight, balance, and control of the hull under the sails in relation to the elements they operate in. The America's Cup competition has been a major field for research and development. Limited by the restrictions of a precise measurement rule, the designers who have produced the 12-Meter yachts used in America's Cup competition since 1958 have still managed to make enough improvements and refinements in sail, rig, gear, and hull shape to develop boats that are slightly faster than their predecessors each time there has been a cup match. Success has been measured in mere seconds per mile, which translates into a tactically commanding advantage of a boat length or two on a course leg of several miles—enough to win races. In the process, the 12-Meter of 1958 looks almost as archaic as a caravel of Columbus alongside the boats developed over the next two decades.

There are no precise, definitive answers to all the development problems because so many variables are involved in the subtle process of getting the best out of a boat. The question is often asked as to whether the hull shape, sails, or skipper and crew is the most important element, and the answer can never be a simple one. No one factor by itself is the answer. Given the ultimate in design and the very best in sails, a poor skipper and/or a crew that executes sloppily can ruin the best efforts of designer and sailmaker. In the same way, the very best sailor in the world is helpless if he is given a clunker to sail, or if his sails are poorly cut and trimmed.

On top of the need for combining all these factors properly, the vagaries of wind, wave, and tide also affect a boat's performance in ever-changing combinations.

All this is why the ultimate answer to how a boat sails and what makes it sail well is a fascinating conundrum that serves as a continuing challenge. No one has ever been able to state truthfully and with confidence that he knows everything there is to know about sailing. An America's Cup designer or skipper, an Olympic champion, or an ocean race winner has to admit that he is always learning, always uncovering new facets, new angles, new avenues of exploration.

These considerations are the ultimate. At the beginning there is still the basic question of how a boat sails that underlies the intricate skein of interdependencies built on top of the basics. One spin in a sailboat is enough to reveal the fact that it will, when adequately handled, proceed downwind, across the wind, and as close to the wind as about 45°, leaving a sector of about 90° out of the total 360° in which direct progress is impossible. Some boats will sail closer than 45° to the wind, and others can't quite make that angle, but it is a basic one for generalization. Inside that sector of 45° on each side of the direction from which the wind is blowing, the sail flaps, or *luffs*, and has no more driving power than a flag rippling in the breeze. If the wind is a sailboat's source of power, as gasoline is to a powerboat or car, and the sails are thought of as the engine, steering a boat into this windward sector is like taking a car or powerboat out of gear. It is only when the wind is coming from enough of an angle on the side to keep a sail from luffing and to exert power on one side of it and make it keep its shape that a sailboat is *in gear*. Obviously, then, progress to a point directly to windward, or anywhere within that 90° sector, must be made in a series of zigzags, like a snake going upstairs.

How is this accomplished? Aside from the rather simple process of blowing straight downhill, what are the elements that combine to make a boat proceed into the other parts of the circle in which operations are possible? How is the power of the wind harnessed so that it doesn't merely tip a boat over or blow it directly to leeward?

The shape of the sail is the key. If a sail were merely a flat plane,

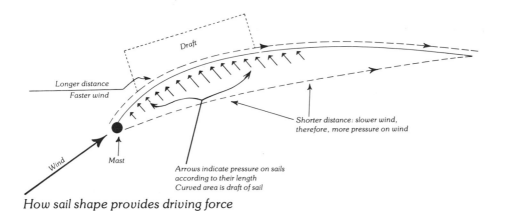

How sail shape provides driving force

like a piece of cardboard, it would only be effective directly downwind, when any surface that offers resistance to the wind transmits its power. A sail is not flat, however. It has an airfoil shape (see diagram) and the principle is the same as the lift of an airplane wing section or the wing of a bird. Air flowing past the curved shape of the sail goes faster on the longer route around the outside of the curve than the air flowing across the inside of it. The faster air, lingering a shorter time in its passage across the sail, exerts less pressure on it than the slower air on the other side. That extra pressure applied to the deepest part of the curve, which is called the draft, has a forward force rather than a straight sideways one. If it is harnessed properly by the trim of the sail, and if the boat is designed properly so that the tipping moment that remains in this sideways force is counteracted and the hull shape responds well to the forward drive of the sail, the boat can be made to proceed at any angle to the wind desired (until you get into the 90° luffing sector).

One sail, as in a catboat rig, can transmit this forward force well, but a single sail becomes difficult to handle in larger boats, and it then is more efficient to split up the sail area into more than one sail, as mentioned in the previous chapter. Not only does a sloop rig permit better staying of the mast, which can be located back toward the middle of the boat in a wider and stronger part of it, but the

Note draft in main and jibs

interaction of the two sails can also increase their efficiency and drive. The jib and mainsail both have draft cut into them by the sailmaker, and the air acts the same way going around the curve, giving both sails forward drive. In addition, the slot between the sails, especially if the jib overlaps the mainsail, increases the speed of the airflow across the back of the main.

Naturally, if this drive is being transmitted to a "shoebox," the result is not going to be very satisfying, and the boat must be an efficient instrument for reacting to the force of the sails. As can be seen from the rundown of hull forms in the previous chapter, there is no one answer to this, and designers are always coming up with new ideas on a hull shape that will provide more speed.

The basics are to keep the boat from tipping too much—overreacting to the sideways force of the wind on the sail, thereby spilling wind and losing some of its force—and to provide the least resistance to forward motion. The tipping force can be counteracted by weight in the boat, either in the form of built-in ballast in the hull or attached to the keel, by the placement of crew weight, or both. In light-centerboard boats without permanent ballast, crew weight has to do it all. In larger, heavier, deeper boats, the boat does most of the work, but crew weight can still be a factor.

The variations in hull form are virtually infinite. A broad, flat hull like a scow's can be extremely fast off the wind but is not good in any kind of sea. A narrow, deep hull can be *seakindly* in rough going but will have too much wetted surface to permit good speeds in light air and in downwind work. Since there is friction, and therefore resistance, between water and the underwater surface of a hull moving through it, the more wetted area there is, the greater the force needed to overcome the resistance. Every boat is therefore a compromise of some sort, a basic consideration that should be kept in mind in every element of a boat. The need for certain qualities will always mean paying a price in certain drawbacks. The designer and owner must decide what compromise suits them best in a given boat. Speed, seaworthiness, comfort, ease of handling, safety, and even looks—each must be balanced against the others according to an owner's needs and the use for which the boat is intended. As examples of ridiculous extremes, you don't race a centerboard scow to Bermuda, and you don't put a deep-hulled sea-going yacht in an inland pond.

Points of Sailing

With a background knowledge of the forces involved in making a sailboat move, the next step is to go into the various points of sailing, the angles in that 270° sector in which sailing is possible.

The three points of sailing are across the wind, or *reaching*; downwind, or *running*; and to a point to windward, or *beating*—with variations on each. Sail trim, crew placement, and steering must be handled differently in each case.

REACHING   is the simplest point of sailing and the easiest. The boat is easy to control, and it is probably the best way for a beginner to gain confidence and get the feel of a boat under sail. A boat is on a reach

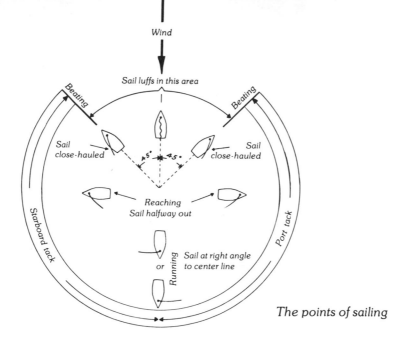

Wind

Sail luffs in this area

Beating

Beating

Sail
close-hauled

Sail
close-hauled

45°   45°

Starboard tack

Port tack

Reaching
Sail halfway out

Running

or

Sail at right angle
to center line

The points of sailing

when the wind is roughly at right angles to the course. On a close reach, the wind is slightly forward of the beam. The boat is said to be on a broad, or quartering, reach when the angle of the wind is aft of the beam. Sail trim calls for the sails to be about halfway out, the maximum distance without causing luffing. There is pressure on the helm down toward the sail, as the boat wants to head up to windward; and this should be counteracted with good, steady counterpressure from the helmsman. Crew weight should be sufficiently to windward to keep the boat on as even a keel as possible. Reaching is the fastest point of sailing. On the centerboard boats, it is usually best to have the board about a quarter to a half down.

RUNNING   Running, when the boat is going directly or almost directly before the wind, requires care in steering and weight placement. The sails are slacked off as far as they will go, with the boom virtually at right angles to the centerline of the boat. The helm will normally not have as much pressure as on a reach, and the boat should be steered carefully so that the wind doesn't come on the other side of the sails suddenly and cause an accidental jibe. It is usually a good idea to put crew weight on both sides of the boat to keep her relatively level. In centerboard boats, the only need for the board might be a small amount to aid steering control. Otherwise, it is just unnecessary wetted surface and drag.

BEATING Beating has more nuances than the other points of sailing, with subtle reactions to the vagaries of the wind an important factor. While on a beat, a boat is sailed as close to the wind as possible without causing the sails to luff, and with the sails trimmed in as tightly as the rig allows.

Crew weight should be placed to keep the boat as level as possible On a well-designed boat with good balance, there should not be heavy helm pressure. Handling the helm while beating takes a sure and delicate touch in reaction to slight changes in wind strength and direction. In centerboarders, the board should be all, or almost all, the way down, depending on depth of water and the balance of the boat.

Reaching is the fastest point of sailing

5

Handling a Boat Under Sail

THE PREVIOUS chapter covered the basic points of sailing, simply stated. If the wind were a steady, constant force in strength and direction, handling the helm would be as easy as steering a car down a straight road, and sail trim could remain virtually the same for long periods of time. The wind, however, is seldom constant for any length of time. It is the single biggest variable in all the intricate web of variables that affect the performance of a sailboat, and an understanding of wind behavior is an absolute prerequisite to success in handling a sailboat in even the simplest day sailing situations, much less a race.

Knowing the Wind

Study of wind vanes, flags, anemometers, and the surface of the water will quickly indicate how unsteady the wind is on even the most normal of days. Across open water, far from land, wind behavior is steadier than it is near shore, where hills, trees, buildings, and land features that change air temperature, such as major highways, parking lots, or concentrations of unshaded buildings, all have an effect on wind patterns. Notice how wind vanes and flags flick to slightly different angles every few moments, and watching an anemometer needle for a few minutes shows how wind strength comes in uneven bursts, or puffs, like the breathing of an asthmatic giant. As an extreme, everyone knows how the wind swirls and eddies in unpredictable gusts in the streets beneath city skyscrapers. Some of this effect is present whenever the wind is approaching you over obstructions of any kind.

Even over open water, unstable air causes changes in the wind. Sailors must remain on the alert for changes in wind behavior at all times and adjust quickly to them. Failure to do so can bring results ranging from simple loss of boat speed to disastrous knockdowns causing a capsize or rig damage.

It sounds simple to say that you should always know which way the wind is blowing, yet unfamiliarity with this is a major cause of difficulty for novices, and even the most experienced sailors can be caught unawares. Just a look at the nearby surface of the water isn't enough, although a good start is the old technique of wetting your finger and holding it up. It actually works.

Depending on where you are, there are other indications to check:

Direction in which surface waves are moving. Be sure you are looking at wind waves and not a leftover cross-chop or a disturbance from tide or current.

Behavior of flags, trees, and smoke. Distant flags or smoke in areas open to unobstructed wind may be better indicators than those around a landlocked harbor.

The movement of low clouds. High ones often move in a different direction from the surface wind.

The feel of the wind against your cheek and ears. Turning your back to the wind until the pressure is equal on both ears.(Long-hairs have a problem here.)

Darker patches on the water and an increase in whitecaps and wind streaks help in indicating new puffs of stronger wind and changes in direction.

The boat should be equipped with some sort of wind indicator as well. A wind sock, feather, or small arrow atop the mast, or the burgee on a cruising boat, is a help, and telltales—small lengths of yarn attached to the mast shrouds and backstay—are even more valuable. On larger boats, electronic equipment can give wind direction and velocity, and most racing boats have a set of telltales near the leading edge of the jib on both sides of the sail. When these line up and flow evenly on both sides of the sail, trim is correct. If the inner ones flutter unevenly, the boat is being sailed too close to the wind. The flutter of the outer ones indicates heading too far off.

Apparent Wind

The movement of the boat herself is another factor in wind direction that must be understood. Obviously the boat's speed and course in relation to the true wind have an effect on the angle at which the wind actually crosses the boat. This is known as *apparent wind*—the way the wind appears to the sailor aboard the boat as it affects the telltales and governs trim of the sails. As an extreme example, imagine a high-speed ocean liner moving at thirty knots in a flat calm. There is no true wind, but there is an apparent wind of thirty knots from dead ahead moving across her. When a vessel's course is at an angle to the wind, which it always is in a sailboat except on a run dead downwind, the apparent wind becomes a change in angle, sometimes small, sometimes quite significant. It is apparent wind, not true wind, that governs sail trim. High-speed sailboats, such as planing monohulls, catamarans, and iceboats, create a much greater change between true and apparent wind than slower ones, and they are trimmed closer a great percentage of the time. Iceboats, which can travel faster than the true wind speed because of minimum friction, are almost always close-hauled no matter what the point of sailing. The effect of the wind on an iceboat's sail creates a force that can drive the boat at these higher speeds because there is almost no resistance between the ice and the boat's runners. As the iceboat's speed increases, the apparent wind strength also increases and adds to the force working on the boat's progress.

This same effect is present in much less dramatic proportions in sailboats moving through or across water. When a puff hits a boat and increases her speed, the angle of apparent wind moves forward and is increased by the boat's faster motion, so that sails must be trimmed accordingly. This is especially noticeable in big powerful boats like 12-Meters or the maxi ocean racers in the seventy-to-eighty-foot range. In moderate breezes under ten knots, as the boat gets up momentum and starts moving, she actually creates her own *wind across the deck,* and boat speed can be equal to or better than true wind speed. Not many boats are that efficient or that powerful, but apparent wind, as the wind you are always sailing in, must therefore always be kept in mind.

Rigging a Boat

Now that we have seen the forces that propel a sailboat and the direction in which it is possible for the boat to sail, the next step is to check out handling a boat in them, the mechanics of rigging, getting underway and maneuvering through the various points of sailing, and returning to base.

Before a boat can be taken sailing, she must be properly equipped and rigged. Many of the specific details depend on the size and type of boat, but there are some general steps that apply to all. From the simplest dinghy up, there are requirements that all boats should meet. There are Coast Guard safety equipment requirements for every class of boat, and those should be known when the boat is acquired. Every boat should have an anchor and line enough for at least 6 to 1 scope in depths of water where anchoring is feasible. Life jackets for each person, some means of bailing (a can on a dinghy, an installed pump on larger boats), and means of auxiliary propulsion—from a paddle to an auxiliary engine—are all necessities.

On most boats, the sails are not left on the spars when the boat is not being used. Be sure that you have the right ones for the boat, and that the battens—slats of wood to give the leech stiffness—are with the sails. Check over halyards, sheets, and other trimming lines to make sure that they are led correctly (and that you understand them). Look for frayed areas that might soon cause trouble. Make sure that all lines are free of snarls and tangles, and ready for operation.

Put the mainsail on the boom first, starting from the mast. Work the slides along the track, or the foot line into the groove of the spar (the two most common systems unless the sail is loose-footed, which it is on some small dinghies). With the tack—the forward end of the foot

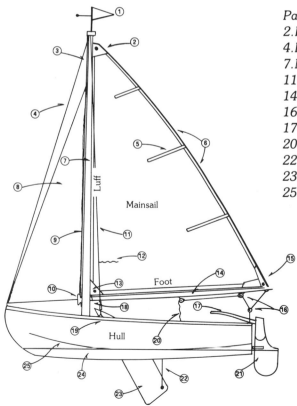

Parts of a sloop: 1. Wind indicator 2. Head of sail 3. Halyard sheave 4. Forestay 5. Batten 6. Leech 7. Mast 8. Jib 9. Halyard 10. Cleat 11. Shroud 12. Telltale 13. Cleat 14. Boom 15. Clew and outhaul 16. Mainsheet blocks and traveler 17. Tiller 18. Gooseneck 19. Rail 20. Mainsheet 21. Rudder 22. Centerboard pennant 23. Centerboard 24. Waterline 25. Chine

made fast at the *gooseneck,* the fitting that joins the boom to the mast—work the sail out to the end by hand, then make sure that there are no puckers or slack spots anywhere along the foot. Make the outer end of the foot—the *clew*—fast to whatever fitting is provided on the end of the boom and take up tension so that the entire foot is taut and smooth.

Next, put the sail on the mast. If slides are used, put them all on in sequence without raising the sail, and attach the halyard to the head of the sail. Make sure it is securely done. Usually a shackle is used, and it is important to check that the shackle is safely closed all the way so that it cannot spring open by accident. If the luff of the sail goes on the mast by sliding rope in a groove, it has to be done while the sail is being hoisted, since there is usually no way of keeping it in the groove unless there is tension on the halyard. The boat must be headed into the wind while hoisting the sail so that there is no pressure on it and to keep it from catching under the shrouds.

In attaching a jib, work from the tack up if the jib has hanks—metal clips on its luff that attach to the headstay. If the jib goes up a slot in the stay, a fairly sophisticated type of fitting on larger racing boats, it must be raised in the act of attachment, just like a luff-in-groove main. When hoisting sails, make sure that the sheets are not cleated or snarled. Sheets are the lines that control sails, not the sails themselves. The word *rope* on a boat refers to the general product; each individual piece of rope is a line—halyards, sheets, guys, downhauls, anchor and mooring lines, and so on.

Make sure that the sails are hoisted under proper tension. Sophisticated racing boats have means of adjusting tension on jib and mainsail luffs with downhauls, winches, etc., but most day sailers and cruising boats have fixed goosenecks on the mainsail and tacks on the jib. All tension is applied via the halyard, and the luffs of both sails should be smoothly taut, with no puckers. A sloppily raised jib with scallops and puckers between the hanks is a giveaway of a novice sailor.

Fittings for attaching and adjusting sails vary greatly from boat to boat, and it is only possible to talk in generalities here, so an important step in starting out in a boat is to become familiar with all these fittings, understanding their function, so that there is no question of how they work when the boat is actually sailing.

Getting Underway

Normal procedure is to raise the main and then the jib, especially if someone must be on the foredeck to help get the boat away from a mooring or pier. In this case, or in raising an anchor, wait until the boat is underway before hoisting the jib. When the sails are properly up, with the halyards in correct tension and cleated, coil the halyard ends by laying the top of each coil in your left hand in a clockwise motion, then pull the inside loop through the coils and fasten it to the cleat with a hitch. Before casting off and beginning to sail, make sure that the tiller or wheel is free and ready for use and that no sheets have become fouled across cleats or other fittings. In a centerboarder,

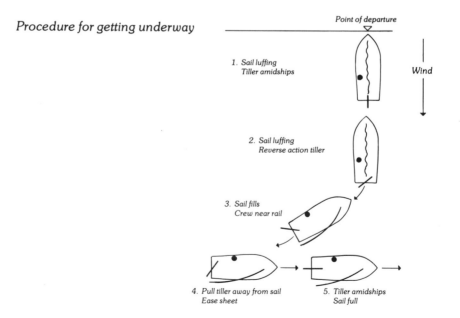

Procedure for getting underway

Point of departure

Wind

1. Sail luffing
   Tiller amidships

2. Sail luffing
   Reverse action tiller

3. Sail fills
   Crew near rail

4. Pull tiller away from sail
   Ease sheet

5. Tiller amidships
   Sail full

have the board at the desired depth for the first point of sailing you expect to be on. Some board depth will be necessary in any case to give better control of the boat while she is gathering way.

Leaving a pier or mooring when there is no current is a relatively simple process. The boat should always be pointed into the wind. If this is impossible where you are, you will have to paddle or motor to a point where the sails may be safely and properly hoisted with the boat head-to-wind. When everything is in readiness, give the boat a shove back from a pier, or let her drift back after dropping a mooring, with the sails luffing and rudder amidships. If you have no crew and no one is on the pier to cast off and give you a shove, you must get back to the helm station as quickly as possible.

While the boat is drifting backward, the rudder acts in reverse, exactly the opposite from the way it does with the boat going forward. Use reverse rudder action to make the bow fall off in the desired direction, after making sure ahead of time that you have a clear path in this course. As the bow falls off, the sails will begin to fill. When they first fill, the effect will be mostly a tipping one, and crew weight should be placed to counteract this. Trim the sails so that they will fill and begin to move the boat forward. That will create forward motion, but it will also tend to bring the bow back into the wind again, since the rudder has little effect while the boat is almost at a standstill in the water. Therefore, after this first trimming action, slack the sails off a bit as the boat gathers way so that the rudder will take over control from the sails. Keep the sails trimmed just enough to give continued forward motion until the boat is moving fast enough for the proper balance between sails and rudder. Then trim the sails correctly for the point of sailing you want to take. Always use the leeward sheet for trimming jibs.

Using partial sail trim in this way is like giving an engine small bursts of power while maneuvering a car or powerboat, waiting until there is sufficient flow of water past the rudder for it to become effective.

Returning to Base

Landing at a pier or picking up a mooring can be a difficult maneuver for a novice, and the steps should be practiced in open water until you become familiar with how the boat acts in given wind strengths. Since a sailboat has no brakes, the only way to simulate braking action is to head into the wind, with sails luffing and all "power" gone, until the boat comes to a stop. The time and distance a boat takes to come to rest is known as *carry*, and you should be familiar with a boat's carrying characteristics before attempting landings.

Test the carry in open water first. Then, when approaching the landing spot, come in on a reach if possible, aiming for a spot at a distance downwind of the landing point just less than the estimated carry. On arriving at this spot, round up sharply and smoothly, head-to-wind, letting the sails luff and making sure the sheets don't foul on cleats, tiller, or other fittings. If you have estimated correctly, the boat will ease up to the pier or mooring at a gradually slowing speed so that there is no great crash against the pier or too much speed for the mooring to be picked up safely. Have someone ready to fend off if you are going to hit the pier too soon. Let the mooring go by if speed is too much for a comfortable pick-up. Even if the crew manages to grab the mooring and make it fast on the bow cleat quickly, the sudden stop when the mooring line takes up against the excessive speed will slue the boat sideways, filling the sails again and making the boat vulnerable to a capsize, since the entire force of filling the sails in this manner will be a tipping one. In a famous disaster in the nineteenth century, the large schooner *Mohawk*, one of the most luxurious racing yachts of the day, was caught with all sails set while at a mooring by a line squall that changed wind direction rapidly and violently. The vessel capsized almost instantly, trapping many of her crew below.

In the opposite case, carry is underestimated, and the boat comes to a stop short of the landing point. That means that the whole maneuver must be repeated unless some quick and vigorous paddling takes place. When the boat comes to a stop with the sails luffing, known as being *in irons* or *in stays,* there is no way to make her go farther to windward, and the procedure used in leaving a point—reversing the tiller and sailing out to get new maneuvering room—must be followed.

Maneuvering in Current

As mentioned, the presence of a current can complicate the above maneuvers. Always check for the presence of current before committing to a maneuver. Look for telltale ripples and *wake* on one side of a buoy, piling, moored boat, or other fixed object. It doesn't take much velocity of current to have considerable effect on a boat's hull. A one-knot current doesn't sound like much until you feel what it can actually do in swinging a boat around.

If the current is in the same direction as the wind, proceed in the same manner as above, only remembering that the carry will be less when wind and current are combined than when wind alone is stopping the boat's progress.

When wind and current are opposed to each other, or the current is running at an angle to the wind, extra problems and difficulties arise. There are so many combinations and variables that no specific rules can be established. The most important point is to be aware of current direction and force so that a plan can be worked out before it is too late. The relative strength of wind and current will govern which one to react to as the primary force. In a strong wind, use it to slow the boat; then lower the sails as quickly as possible before the current slues the boat around, making the sails fill. Sometimes it is better to make an approach against the current downwind, gradually lowering the sail so that just enough speed is maintained to stem the current until the landing is made. In a sloop, killing one sail early can be a help. In getting underway, partial use of sails to clear the area and reach a spot open enough for hoisting them all the way usually works. Formulating a plan ahead of time after analyzing the situation is the best way to handle maneuvering in current.

All this close-in maneuvering involves only a small fraction of the time spent sailing. While underway, the boat is on one of the three points of sailing, and the techniques for each should be learned, as well as for altering from one point to the other and bringing the wind from one side of the boat to the other by one of two methods: *tacking* or *jibing* (sometimes spelled *gybing*).

Reaching

As stated, reaching is the simplest point of sailing and usually the fastest. There is a tendency to sit back and let the boat have her head without paying too much attention to the finer points, and it is true that that is the most relaxing point of sailing. There are techniques, however, and the normal changes in wind strength and direction will also call for some adjustment. It is also a good time for getting the feel of the boat and of her helm, learning the balance and the amount of helm necessary.

As mentioned above, the sails should be about halfway out, just short of the point where luffing begins—it always begins at the leading edge, or luff, of the sail, and the helmsman's eye should never stray too far from this key area. The helm will have a lively pull toward the sail. If the helm is released, the boat will rapidly round up toward the wind on her own, a built-in safety factor. That is a good time to become familiar with the forces at work on a sailboat. Once the right amount of pressure on the helm is learned through experimentation, adjustment of sail trim can come next. When the sail is trimmed without changing course, the boat will tend to tip more and slow down as the flow of wind across both sides of the sail is being equalized, and the sail is *stalling*. The sail should be slacked until luffing begins and then trimmed back in until the moment luffing stops for optimum reaching trim. It should then be tended for any adjustment necessary for changes in wind direction and strength. Remember that the faster the boat moves, the more the apparent wind comes forward, calling for tighter trim on the sail. When a puff eases up, the sail should again be slacked. The helmsman can make some adjustment to wind shifts by alterations of course, but excessive steering slows a boat, and sail trim is the preferred method.

In centerboard boats, roughly half-board is a rule of thumb while on a reach. Too much board will increase wetted surface and tend to add weather helm, while not enough board will make the boat slide sideways. Some weather helm is good and, as mentioned, a safety factor, though too much weather helm puts unnecessary strain on the helmsman. A poorly balanced boat might have *lee helm*, a tendency to head away from the wind if left to herself, an annoying trait and a safety hazard. Sometimes a well-balanced boat will have a lee helm in very light air that can be corrected by moving crew weight around and that will disappear as soon as the wind increases.

Running

Running before the wind is also a relatively easy point of sailing, especially if the wind is moderate and steady, but it is the point of sailing that can get a novice in the most trouble if not done carefully and properly. To go onto a run from a reach, slack the sail and head the boat off, away from the wind direction. Be sure you know what the direction is so that you don't steer so far off the wind that it gets behind the sail and causes it to flip across rapidly and with great force in what is known as an "accidental jibe." In a light boat, this can cause a capsize, and in ballasted boats, an accidental jibe can mean a dismasting or at least some damage to rig and sails.

On a run, most boats have some amount of weather helm, especially catboats and cat-rigged dinghies. Counteracting this takes some effort. In light boats, weight placement is important. It should normally be distributed evenly on each side of the boat, so that there is no angle of heel. Actually, for best rudder action, a slight heel to windward, away from the sail, is preferable in running. The only need for the centerboard to be down in any amount is to aid steering control. If this is not necessary, the board can be all the way up to reduce wetted surface.

Wave action can affect steering on a run. In a good breeze, with considerable wave action, the helmsman must anticipate the way oncoming waves tend to kick the stern around, producing what is known as *yaw*, and it takes some experience to handle this situation properly.

When a spinnaker is being used, which is the case in most racing boats on anything from a reach to a dead run, trim of the spinnaker and constant tending of it is of utmost importance. Details of sail handling and trim will be discussed in Part II. On sloops without a spinnaker, the mainsail blankets the jib, and it is good practice to wing out the jib on the other side with some sort of pole.

In any event, the first consideration on a run is to avoid getting *by the lee*: with the wind at an angle across the stern that puts it behind the sail and leads to a jibe.

Beating

As mentioned before, beating to windward is the most sophisticated point of sailing and the hardest one for the novice to grasp. Its nuances and fine points are varied and relatively complex, though the basics are not. Most races at the club and regional level are won by superior performance to windward, but that is not necessarily so at the top international level. When racing sailors have become expert enough to reach that level, they are all almost equally good on a beat, and skill in the fine points of gaining extra speed on reaches and runs becomes equally important. For the newcomer,

Beating is the most sophisticated point of sailing; note use of crew weight

however, acquiring the feel of making a boat go to windward efficiently is the major step toward becoming an accomplished helmsman.

Awareness of wind direction and the ever-present shifts, lifts, headers, and puffs is vital to windward sailing. Here all the indicators are checked constantly: telltales, masthead fly, indications on the water surface, and the feel of the wind against your cheek and ears. Sail by watching the luff of the major sail—usually the jib is more important than the main while on a beat in a boat with headsails.

The sails should be trimmed in as far as possible. Individual rigs vary, but the main boom should be somewhere between the centerline of the boat and the leeward rail, and the jib should be flat against the leeward shrouds along the leeward rail. Crew weight should be to windward to keep the boat as flat as possible. This applies in everything from a light centerboard to a maxi ocean racer, unless the air is very light. Then some weight to leeward, allowing the boat to heel slightly, helps the sails to keep their shape. In a good breeze, allowing the boat to heel too far spills wind out of the sail and permits the tipping force to become more important than the forward driving force. Centerboards should use full, or nearly full, board, depending on the boat's balance.

Some boats are balanced so well that they virtually sail themselves to windward with very little pressure on the helm, but it is more common to have a slight weather helm, so that the boat tends to head up until the sails luff if there is no counterpressure on the wheel or tiller. Don't fight this tendency. When a puff hits, increasing boat speed, and the apparent wind increases and moves forward, the boat will point up by herself, which is where you want to go, since the object, while on a beat, is to gain distance in the direction from which the wind is blowing. Let the boat do it until you detect the beginning quiver of a luff in the sail you are sailing by. Then hold the helm firm and keep the boat steady on that course until there is another change in wind strength and/or direction. If this is done correctly, the windward telltale will be pointing in at a slight angle to the centerline of the boat, toward the helm station. If the boat is held off and not allowed to head as high as she wants to go, the telltale will point in toward the mast, and the tipping force will be greater. If reaction to these changes is correct, a good course to windward usually follows a scalloped pattern.

Tacking

So far, we have been discussing points of sailing with the wind on the same side of the boat. To change it, to go from one tack to another, can be done in two ways: tacking or jibing. (A boat is always on a tack when the sails are full. It is *on starboard tack* if the wind is coming across the starboard side and *on port tack* when the wind is on that side. On a direct downwind run, the side the mainsail is on determines the tack. If it is out to port, the boat is on starboard tack.)

Tacking, also called *coming about*, is easier and also safer, at least for the novice, and is usually done more frequently than jibing. In tacking, the wind is brought from one side of the boat to the other by swinging the bow through the direction of the wind. In jibing, the wind crosses the stern in being brought to the opposite side.

Since the sails luff and lose power when the boat's bow is head-to-wind, tacking can be done under control, with a relatively slow transfer of pressure from one side of the sails to the other. In jibing, the mainsail goes from full on one tack to full on the other tack with a slam-bang action, and the sudden shift of pressure can cause trouble if the maneuver is not carefully controlled.

To go through the procedure for tacking, let's assume the boat is close-hauled on the starboard tack, and the time has come to change to the port tack. Making sure that all is in readiness, the helmsman says, "Ready about," as a warning of the maneuver he is about to begin. Then, to start the move, he says, "Hard alee," as he pushes the tiller or turns the wheel. This is an old sailing-ship term meaning that the helm, specifically a tiller, has been put down to leeward, toward the sail, to make the boat head into the wind. In wheel steering, of course, the wheel is turned away from the sail, but the term still suffices as the standard signal for effecting a tack. To be technical in wheel steering, you could say, "Hard over," but all sailors are used to "Hard alee" as the traditional call.

The boat will begin a swing into the wind, and the sails will start to luff, first just breaking at the luff, then flapping for their entire width as the wind pressure equalizes on both sides. The rudder should be kept over until the bow swings through the eye of the wind and the wind begins to come across the port bow. As the swing approaches 45° off the wind on the port tack, the helm should be gradually eased amidships so that the boat can be steadied on course as the sails begin to fill on this new angle.

In tacking from close-hauled to close-hauled, it is often not necessary to tend the mainsheet, but jib trim should be shifted to the new leeward sheet, trimming it in just as the boat steadies on her new heading. (This need not be done if the boat is equipped with a self-trimming jib, one with a boom, called a *club*, on its foot, and a sheet

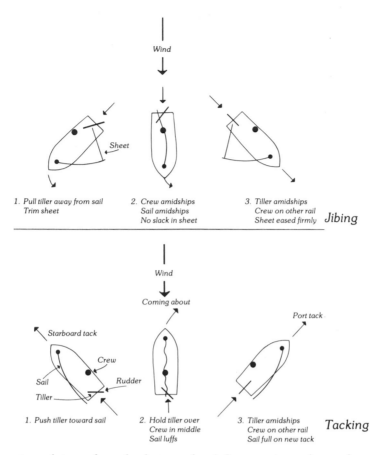

Wind

1. Pull tiller away from sail
   Trim sheet

2. Crew amidships
   Sail amidships
   No slack in sheet

3. Tiller amidships
   Crew on other rail
   Sheet eased firmly *Jibing*

Wind

Coming about

Starboard tack

Crew

Port tack

Sail

Rudder

Tiller

1. Push tiller toward sail

2. Hold tiller over
   Crew in middle
   Sail luffs

3. Tiller amidships
   Crew on other rail
   Sail full on new tack *Tacking*

rigged to a foredeck traveler.) In coming about from farther off the wind than close-hauled, the sheets should be gradually trimmed to keep slack out of them as the bow swings into the wind, and then eased off under control while squaring away on the new tack. In all cases, crew weight should be shifted in rhythm with the tack so that it is amidships while the bow is head-to-wind and on the new windward side as the sails begin to fill. If you have been reaching or running in a centerboarder, with little or no board down, add some board depth while tacking, or the boat will not round up properly.

Tacking is a question of good timing. If the boat is slammed across the wind too quickly, the crew may not have time to shift weight and trim the jib properly, and the boat could stall out. If she is brought into the wind too timidly, she might lose way and not carry through the luffing point. If she refuses to swing through and is stuck in the wind with the sails luffing helplessly, she is in that condition we have seen, known as *in irons* or *in stays*. Hard rudder action might save the situation, and the jib can sometimes be backed in a sloop, holding it out to windward on the old windward side, to make the bow swing. If the boat has been slow in stays but finally does fall away on the desired tack, the rudder will be ineffective until some way is gathered. As the sails fill on the new tack, therefore, they will make the bow fall way off to leeward and will have added tipping force. Sheets should be partially slacked to prevent this and let the boat gather way gradually, making the rudder effective again.

If these methods fail and the boat remains in stays and starts to drift backwards, reverse the rudder action to make the bow fall off correctly. Once it does fall off, the same situation as above, with the rudder ineffective, will result and should be handled in the same way.

In general, heavier boats and boats with long, shallow keels tack more slowly than lightweight centerboarders or fin keel boats, and they should be *sailed* through, coming about with good way on, rather than *put about* with a quick flip of the helm.

Jibing

To set up a jibing maneuver, the helmsman first says, "Stand by to jibe," and then calls, "Jibe-o," as he actually starts the move. To get used to jibing, it is a good idea to practice in moderate air so that mistakes will not cause rigging damage or a capsize, getting the feel and rhythm of how to handle the maneuver in easy conditions. Even experienced sailors jibe with some trepidation in heavy winds, always with the utmost care and concentration.

Since, in jibing, the wind is going to shift from one side of the sail to the other in one big slam, everything possible must be done to minimize this quick alteration of force. Timing and control are even more important than in coming about. If there is need for a rapid change of tack in an emergency, jibing is naturally the quicker method unless the boat is close-hauled and hard on the wind.

Before starting a jibe, the helmsman must make sure that everything is in readiness, with the crew all set to handle each task. For example, in a boat with running backstays, movable ones that are set up on the windward side on each tack, the backstay must be eased forward and the one on the other side readied for setting up before the jibe begins. Many a boom has been broken when that step is forgotten.

As the helm is put over, with a tiller pulled away from the mainsail or a wheel turned toward it, the mainsheet should be trimmed steadily so that there is never any slack in it. That will keep the boom from riding up and slashing over in an uncontrolled motion that can result in a disaster known as *goosewing jibe*. In this, the boom swings up so high, allowing the sail to belly forward, that the belly in the sail can wrap around the mast, causing a tangle that could rip the sail or damage the rig.

Keeping the slack out of the mainsheet, bringing the boom steadily inboard as the boat swings to her new heading, also reduces the distance that the boom will swing in a hard slam when the wind suddenly gets behind the sail. If the sail is trimmed in coordination with the swing of the boat, the distance of the sudden slam-over is reduced, and its force is minimized. If the sail is not trimmed at all, and the boom is allowed to whip over suddenly from all the way out on one tack to all the way out on the other, the boom crosses with dangerous momentum, and the shock of its fetching up at the other end of the jibe is strong, sudden, and capable of carrying away rigging and fittings. That is why accidental jibes should be avoided. Also, there is more danger of the slack in the sheet fouling on a cockpit fitting—or someone's head—in its rapid swing across the boat. All crew members should be very careful to duck below the boom's orbit during a jibe.

In a properly controlled jibe, with the sail trimmed in coordination with the swing of the boat, the arc of uncontrolled crossover is short, and the release of the sheet on the new tack should also be controlled all the way out to the desired trim for the new tack. Since the sail wants to swing out rapidly after the crossover, the sheet-tender should be careful not to let it run loosely through the hands, or a bad rope burn can result. It should be eased out under continuous control. That is relatively easy in a light boat. In a larger one, or in heavy winds in any boat, it may be necessary to snub the sheet around a winch or cleat to reduce the pressure on the sheet-tender's hands. Failure to ease the sheet quickly enough is also wrong, for the sudden tipping force will be a strong one. Again, timing is the key.

During a jibe, crew weight should be shifted in rhythm with the crossover of the sail. It should be mainly amidships as the boom swings over and then quickly shifted to the new windward rail to counteract the force of the sudden filling of the sail.

In a boat with headsails, the jib is not a real problem during a jibe, since it is almost completely blanketed by the mainsail, and there are no heavy forces on it. Jibing a spinnaker requires special techniques that will be discussed in the chapter on racing.

Jibing takes practice. Once the rhythm and coordination of a controlled jibe are mastered, as the climax to familiarization with the rudiments of reaching, running, beating, and coming about, a sailor has learned the ABCs of sailing and should be able to take a boat to any desired destination in normal conditions. As stated before, however, this is only the groundwork on which an unending repertoire of skills can be built. There will be new nuances and subtleties to sailing during every subsequent sail. The learning process, and the challenge of it, never ends.

Right away, for example, there is an awareness that sailing is not aways carried on in ideally pleasant conditions of smooth water and

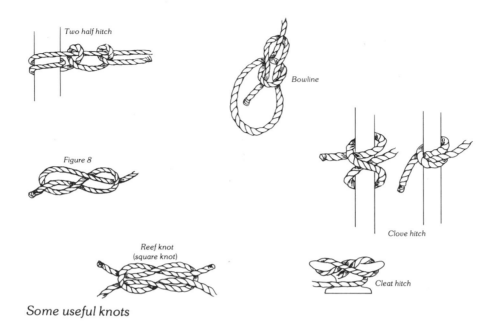

Two half hitch

Bowline

Figure 8

Clove hitch

*Reef knot
(square knot)*

Cleat hitch

Some useful knots

breezes from eight to twelve knots. Sometimes there is very little wind, and sometimes there is almost too much or definitely too much. What about handling boats in these less-than-ideal conditions?

Sailing in Light Air

Light-air sailing can be frustrating but seldom presents real problems unless you are becalmed offshore and unable to get home on schedule. Patience and concentration are important. Wind behavior must be detected from the slightest indications: a streak of air darkening the water, a flutter of a telltale, the faint caress of air on cheek or ear, even the drift of cigarette smoke. Look for signs and be ready to react to them. Just the slightest shove from a stray zephyr that starts a boat moving may set up enough momentum and apparent wind to keep way on.

Once this happens, sail the boat loosely, with sheets slacked and luff and foot of the main eased a bit if they are adjustable. Use crew weight to heel the boat to leeward slightly so that the sails' own weight can keep them full, holding what air they have. Then avoid moving crew weight at all, if possible; in fact, don't even sneeze. Keep the boat in the groove and moving. Any quick shift of weight will throw the wind out of the sails and kill the boat's way. In a centerboarder, board depth can be reduced to cut down wetted surface, since there is little lateral force. If possible, put lightweight sheets on jibs, spinnakers, etc., so that the weight of the sheet does not make the sail sag and spill air. Keep rudder action to a minimum and don't make any sudden radical changes in rudder angle. It is illegal to "scull" a boat with the rudder when racing, but this action—a quick, continuous flipping back and forth—can be helpful in negotiating the last few feet to a mooring or pier.

The boat's balance may change in light air, with a lee helm developing; that can be corrected by placement of crew weight, change in centerboard depth, or change in sail trim. Make as few tacks and jibes as possible; those maneuvers will spill the wind and you must start all over again to get it back. Above all, be patient. It is impossible to sail in light air unless you are.

Sailing in Heavy Air

Work up gradually to sailing in really heavy air. Gain confidence in solid but manageable breezes before going out in really heavy air. To

Patience is required in light-air sailing

Work up gradually to the challenges of heavy-weather sailing

the newcomer, anything over eighteen knots can seem like too much air, and even experienced sailors have to watch themselves when it gets into the twenties and thirties. First of all, you must have confidence in boat and gear. Old sails, frayed lines, and loose or corroded rigging will not stand up to the forces of heavy-weather sailing. Be sure you have proper life jackets and safety equipment, and you will enjoy yourself more if you have light, sturdy, flexible foul-weather gear especially designed for sailboat crews. If the mainsail can be reefed by rolling the boom, by tying reef points, or by other methods, which vary by the boat, you should do so. Choose the smallest jib if there is an option.

Heavy air is always gusty. It may feel all right for a short spell, but then an extra puff will hit like the one-two punch of a boxer, and this is when you must be ready. The very first onslaught of a gust is the most dangerous time. It usually packs the most weight of all and is often from a different direction. Watch for wind streaks, dark patches on the water, and heavier whitecaps close together as signs of an advancing puff. Avoid starting a tack or jibe when one is approaching. Try to wait for a lull between puffs to make maneuvers.

Crew weight is naturally of great importance, especially in small boats, and it should be properly placed at all times: well to windward on beats and reaches, especially in a strong puff, and aft and evenly distributed on runs. The sails are safety valves as well as power sources in heavy air, and judicious slacking to spill wind is a major safety factor. Slacking and heading up slightly, or *feathering*, a technique that requires experience and feel, can nurse a boat through heavy puffs that would be too much for her with a completely full sail. If caught with too much sail, carry a luff in the main at all times— possibly in the jib, too—and use the leech area only for power.

Watch the waves and don't fight them. Rather than slamming into them, watch their pattern, which always includes variations in wave size. Ease the boat over the bigger ones, then feather up through the smaller ones.

There are many tricks to heavy-weather sailing. Each boat has her

Watch the waves and don't fight them in heavy air

own peculiarities, so that experience is all-important, but the above are some basics to remember.

Those are the fundamentals of handling a boat under sail. If you have mastered them—and you can only master them if you combine actual experience afloat with theory—there are many ways in which they can be applied. Perhaps you would like to stop with the basics, aware of how a boat can be sailed from one point to another and able to accomplish it in reasonable time and with reasonable expectation of being safe and successful in these limited aims. Many people enjoy being afloat on these terms, content to keep the boat moving adequately without worrying about the nuances that improve performance. Feet on the gunwale and beer in hand, literally or figuratively, they are satisfied with that level and just happy to be afloat. I must admit to this attitude on certain occasions. With the sun warm and the breeze gentle, I am content to loaf along for the sheer joy of being there and the relaxation of not worrying about much of anything.

That type of involvement as a permanent attitude means a casual approach that can become bland and repetitive. Not many remain in this vegetable-like state ad infinitum. There is so much to the complex art of sailing a boat that it is hard to avoid the challenge. Even those who have no desire for competition can become deeply involved in the whole fabric of keeping a sailboat going. Correct gear and fittings, and their maintenance and operation, hold a fascination for the gadgeteer type. And, since the weather cannot be relied upon to be bland and moderate forever, there are seamanship skills that should be learned by anyone who spends any amount of time afloat.

Many more sailors become involved with cruising and day sailing than with competition. Racing is the only reason for going sailing for an active, athletically inclined minority, but noncompetitive sailing has many more devotees. Cruising is a whole way of life that requires certain arts and skills and a deep involvement with a boat as a machine for living. While ultimate boat speed may not be the main goal, the dedicated cruising yachtsman does require good enough performance to make a sailing passage an enjoyable challenge. He should know more than the simple basics of reaching, running, and beating. He still must know the best sail trim and combination of sails for given wind strengths and points of sailing, and he must know what his boat is capable of in meeting various conditions of wind and sea. The fine points of cruising are covered in Part III.

Racers may be in a numerical minority, but they are so involved, and so dedicated, that their impact is great on the whole sailing scene. Most clubs and organizations are run by racing sailors, and they are the ones who get the headlines in the newspapers and boating magazines. As a contrast to the feet-on-the-gunwale sailor, the racer is instinctively competitive. As soon as he gets in something that moves, he starts thinking about moving faster than someone else.

That fosters competition in everything from dinghies to ocean racers. The basic skills discussed in this chapter must be refined and developed for the rest of one's life for continued success in racing. Part II is devoted to the many aspects of sailboat racing.

RACING

__6

The Organization of Sailboat Racing

IT IS SAFE to say that sailboat racing is the most complex form of recreational competition man has ever devised. It need not be expensive, but it can become the most expensive of sports in certain forms, such as the America's Cup and distance racing. Its demands on the participants match those of any other sport in depth and variety, if not in physical strength and certain types of dexterity. Then, beyond the human skills that must be acquired and developed, and the rules of the game—certainly as complicated as any other form of contest that is basically a race, as opposed to team sports like football—the equipment is by far the most complex. Even the simplest dinghy is a relatively complicated instrument compared to skis, racquets, balls, or golf clubs, and a maxi ocean racer is an unbelievably sophisticated machine.

In this complexity lies the true fascination of the sport. Because of its multiple facets, there is never a plateau of knowledge, nor even a ceiling on it. New techniques, new pieces of gear, new materials, and new concepts in design are continuously changing sailboat racing. As we previously pointed out, no one can validly claim to know everything there is to know about the sport. Yesterday's champion, who seemed to have every technique and trick at his fingertips, must accept the fact that younger challengers are continuously developing new ideas that outmode the accepted techniques of even the recent past.

The development of new winners is not dependent on advances in physical strength or size, however. Sailing skill is not based on any set of physical requirements, and almost everyone has the basic physical equipment to be a racing skipper. In general, age, size, strength, and sex are not important. True, in certain kinds of sailing, weight and physical strength are factors, but there is a place in sailing competition for almost every physical type. Given an equal boat in which weight is not a factor, a ten-year-old girl can beat someone with the physical capabilities of a pro football player.

Sailors can be made—up to a point. Learning everything concrete there is to know about racing can produce a contestant who can compete at the very highest levels, but there is an X factor in it, too, as at the top level of every skill. Millions can play the piano well to expertly, but there are very few Paderewskis or Rubinsteins. Golf has its Bobby Jones or Jack Nicklaus, tennis its Tilden, and so on. That extra something in finesse and skill, that indefinable touch, is also there in a few sailors. It can be approached, but never quite learned by rote. As I mentioned before, the very best sailor in the world can be handicapped by poor equipment. If any factor is weak—boat, sails or crew—he can be beaten despite all the X factors imaginable. Yet certain helmsman do have that touch, that extra something, that gets

Sailing has a few superstars like Bus Mosbacher

the extra seconds of speed out of a boat, that gets the most out of every vagary of breeze, and that reacts instinctively in the right way in the split second that resolves a critical situation.

Super skippers like Sherman Hoyt, Bus Mosbacher, Buddy Melges, or Paul Elvstrom are extremely rare, however, and many others can reach the very best levels of competition with good expectations of success. One reason for this is that sailboat racing offers so many different forms of competition under the overall umbrella of the term. The two major variations are one-design racing and handicap racing, but each of these has many forms. In one-design competition, the boats are all from the same design and the specifications for construction and equipment are also the same. Theoretically, therefore, the boats are even and the results of a race depend on the skill of the skipper and crew and their ability to handle wind and sea conditions. Actually, one-design racing is not that simple, and there are many ramifications, but the basic premise is that the boats are equal.

Handicap racing permits boats of different size and specifications to compete against one another. Here they are theoretically equalized by some form of handicapping system that gives time allowances to supposedly slower boats. There are many forms of handicap racing.

Although it is possible for all ages, all sizes, and both sexes to compete on even terms, there are competitions for various categories based on one of these qualifications.

Virtually all sailing competition is conducted under the same set of rules. The sailing rules—revised, amended, and reworked every few years—are promulgated by an organization known as the International Yacht Racing Union, made up of delegates from the official national bodies of all countries sponsoring organized sailboat racing. Its central office is at 60 Knightsbridge, London, SW1X 7JX, England. A subcommittee of IYRU works on rule revisions and updating, and the complete book of rules is a pamphlet of about seventy pages. The United States IYRU affiliate is the United States Yacht

Buddy Melges, coaxing a scow throught light air here, is another rarely talented skipper

Racing Union, 10 Defenders Row, Goat Island, Newport, Rhode Island 02840, and the rules and other USYRU publications may be obtained from that office.

No one should take part in sailboat racing without a knowledge of these rules. While the pamphlet is lengthy, and no one could be expected to memorize the whole thing, certain basics must become familiar, and everyone should be aware of the general provisions covering all situations that can develop on a course. The most important basic rules are that the starboard tack boat, the boat being overtaken, and the leeward boat have the right of way. The rules are so complicated, due to the great variety of situations that can arise, that many books have been written to interpret them, and appeals of decisions on the rules are also published in a separate USYRU book, which serves as a commentary.

Sailing is peculiar in that it is a sport in which officials are not directly at the scene of the contest, as is a football referee blowing a whistle and walking off fifteen yards, or an umpire thumbing out the baseball runner at first base. Most sailing fouls occur out of sight of the race committee because of the way a racing fleet spreads over a course, and fouls are determined after the race is over through the machinery of a skipper filing a protest against another boat if he thinks a foul has been committed. The protest is then heard by a protest committee, with each crew testifying as to their actions. In baseball it would be as though the ump met the first baseman and the runner in the locker room after the game and listened to each one in turn argue whether the runner was safe or out. It is an unavoidable weakness of the sport, and the system depends on the honesty of the contestants, as well as their ability to reconstruct an incident accurately. Inequities sometimes result, but sailors who are consistently dishonest or inaccurate in testifying at protest hearings seem to earn a reputation after a while. In most cases, a boat that is found to have committed a foul is disqualified and receives no points for the race, but there are some systems of graduated and partial penalties. In addition, there is a provision, optional for the sponsoring organization, that allows a boat that has admittedly fouled to make two complete turns before continuing the race, something like a yardage penalty in football. This is known as the *720 rule,* since two complete turns make 720°.

In addition to covering fouls of contact or interference, the rules also specify starting and finishing procedures, types of courses, and many other administrative items.

The IYRU and USYRU are the broad governing bodies under which sailing competition is organized, but they do not sponsor or conduct many regattas except for special championship events. Most competition is organized at the local level, with yacht clubs sponsoring and running the races. Most yacht clubs, but not all, are members of Yacht Racing Associations that have some geographical factor in common, such as a state, a body of water, or a local region. Typical YRAs are those of Massachusetts Bay, Long Island Sound, Barnegat Bay, southern California, the Inland Lakes, San Francisco Bay, and Texas, to name just a few. The YRAs belong to the USYRU and are grouped in eight regions throughout the country. Canada has a similar set-up, as do most sailing countries around the world. Through the framework of this machinery, USYRU conducts individual championships for senior men (Mallory Cup), senior women (Adams Cup), match racing (Prince of Wales Bowl), single-handers (O'Day Trophy), and various categories of juniors. Club and regional eliminations lead to national finals, all in boats provided for by the clubs conducting the races, sailed round-robin in as many races as there are entrants.

Although those are important events and the winners have survived a long route of eliminations to achieve them, they are only one form of championship competition, and the number of participants is small compared to the sailors engaged in local competition in their own boats. The great bulk of sailboat racing is conducted by local clubs. In addition, some public municipal sailing facilities, marinas, class organizations, and boat manufacturers hold races in which the contestants need not be club members. Some distance races are sponsored by organizations formed just for the purpose.

Club racing is conducted under the general IYRU and USYRU rules in most cases, but local conditions may govern setting of courses, schedules, point systems, and other optional variables. Most one-design racing takes place over relatively short courses with the racing completed in daylight hours. Usually a series of races over a season, month, or regatta week decides the winner. Some clubs also hold races for varied fleets competing under a handicap system in day races. Most distance races, taking overnight, a weekend, or longer, are handicap affairs.

Entirely separate from clubs and the USYRU, sailboat racing is also organized by one-design class associations. There are more than a hundred such groups, some administered by owners of the boats, some by manufacturers or designers. Some class associations control the plans for their boat, selling them to professional or home builders for a fee, while control of other designs remains with the designer or manufacturer. These associations set up official specifications for the boats as to measurements, sail plan and area, and authorized equipment, and sometimes such items as crew weight. Those class regulations must be followed any time the boat is in a race, but the classes themselves usually confine race sponsorship to class regional and national or international championships, held in cooperation with local clubs or facilities.

No governing body oversees the various one-design associations. Anyone who starts a class and can find enough kindred souls can just form an organization. One-design classes go back to the Star boat, developed in 1907 and still going strong after many changes of rig and specificatons. Among the better-known classes are the Snipe, Thistle, Lightning, Blue Jay, Inland Lake Scow, 420, 470, Soling, Comet, Rhodes 19, Hobie Cats, Laser, Sunfish, and Flying Scot.

Perhaps the most intense competition in one-design racing is in the Olympics. Sailing races are part of each Olympics, and the official classes have varied over the years, including the Star, Dragon, Flying Dutchman, 6- and 5.5-Meters, and more lately the Finn, Tempest, Soling, 470, and Tornado catamaran. An Olympic Sailing Committee, in cooperation with USYRU, administers the eliminations and qualifying regattas of competition in the Games.

In 1973, USYRU, then known as the North American YRU, established a National Sailing Center at Association Island, New York, on Lake Ontario. Many Olympic trial regattas, as well as class championships and USYRU regattas, are held at that facility, where USYRU provides an expert race committee to conduct the competitions.

That is the rather fragmented framework through which sailboat racing is conducted. The techniques of racing, the conduct of races by committees, and the special characteristics of the different kinds of racing are covered in the following chapters.

The Comet is an example of a one-design class of longstanding popularity

__7

Racing on Closed Courses

SAILBOAT RACES run the gamut from sprints around an inner harbor in dinghies to long-distance grinds across oceans or even around the world. By far the greatest number of contestants engage in racing on closed courses: *around the buoys*, with start and finish in the same area over distances that allow the race, or group of races, to be finished in the daylight hours of one day. Most of those races are in one-design classes, but some handicap racing is also done over closed courses.

In this chapter, we will go over the basic techniques of this kind of racing. They provide a foundation for proceeding further into the complex world of tactics, rules, techniques, and equipment. Book after book has been written on each one of these phases, and the learning process continues ad infinitum for novice and expert alike. The library of a serious racing sailor should house a long shelf of these specialized tomes, and magazine articles continue to develop new themes, but their subject matter must be built on the basics.

A combination of factors determines racing success. Each has its importance. No one can be ignored and no single one can bring success without the others. There is an interdependence based on coordination. We have already mentioned, in Chapter 4, that this combination consists of a good boat, good sails, good crew, and good skipper. Weakness in any one can offset excellence in the others, and part of being a good skipper lies in making sure that all these elements are combined. The boat and her equipment should give maximum speed potential. The skipper and crew should use this speed potential in the best possible way. Sounds simple, doesn't it?

But it is not simple, and therein lies the appeal of sailboat racing. It is an involvement for much more than the time spent on the race course. The dedicated sailor devotes many more hours to improving his racing skills and chances of success. Study of the rules comes first. Don't race until you have them firmly in mind, and occasional refreshers help in maintaining familiarity. Keep studying those technical articles in the boating magazines and books by experts that appear in a steady stream. New ideas pop up all the time, as well as new slants on familiar subjects.

Reading is helpful, but practice afloat is even more important. The more time spent afloat, the more natural sailing becomes. The "feel" of the boat and her special characteristics and capabilities become second nature. Put her through tacks, jibes, and mark roundings until the rhythm of these maneuvers is established and timing becomes almost automatic. Get to know her carry, her turning circle, her time through a tack, the amount of weather helm on each point of sailing, and the best distribution of crew weight. Much of this can be done solo, but it is also good practice to brush with other boats for comparison. In discussing tuning later on, we will see how this can be especially important.

Maintenance

Maintenance rates high as a between-race activity. Poor equipment has lost many a race, and the care and feeding of a racing sailboat is a continuous project. Some skippers love the manual work and the messing with gadgets; others consider it a bore and a chore. Either way, it should be done. Condition of the bottom comes first. Most one-designs are dry-sailed—stored on land and launched only for racing, offering ample opportunity for work on the surface. Elimination of gouges and scratches, and constant smoothing and polishing of the finish, whether it be fiberglass or wood, pays dividends in lack of friction afloat. Rudders and centerboards should be free from nicks and scars on leading and trailing edges, and uniformly smooth. Between races, surfaces should be washed free of dirt, sand, etc. Bottoms of wet-sailed boats should naturally be checked for fouling and cleaned often with a soft cloth or brush.

Care of sails is very important. They should be rinsed often if used in salt water and folded carefully for stowage, to prevent creases and wrinkles from forming. Rips and tears should be repaired when first detected, and lashing on grommets and stitching in stress areas like tack and clew should be inspected often. Between seasons, sails should be returned to the sailmaker for checking and renovation, and possibly recutting if they have not been giving top performance. Action photos of how they set can help the sailmaker in analyzing them.

All rigging and equipment should be kept in top working order, lubricated and cleaned so that there is no jamming or freezing of moving parts. Lines should be checked for fraying or other weaknesses. Continuous attention to small details as they crop up prevents major overhaul problems after a period of neglect. A racing boat is a piece of machinery, and to be effective she must be maintained in top condition.

Tuning

The word *tuning* has a mystique for the racing sailor, as if it were the complete answer for racing success, known only by real insiders. Tuning is definitely important, but it is far from the only answer, and

Tuning involves proper relation of sails and spars; note controlled mast bend here

the mystique really isn't so mysterious. Much depends on the sophistication of the boat. Setting up a 12-Meter for America's Cup competition does take a tremendous amount of adjustment. It continues all summer and is never really completed. The average one-design racing boat presents no such problem. Tuning can be accomplished in a few relatively simple moves. The basic purpose is to adjust the rigging so that there is the best interplay of the sails, and so that the boat is balanced correctly for the most effective sailing. Each class has its own tricks and requirements, and no single set of ABCs applies to every boat. There was a time when tuning meant making sure that the mast was straight, but so many classes now have controlled bend that this definition no longer applies. Straightness, rake, or bend should be in the correct manner for the sails. Normally there should be a slight amount of weather helm when going to windward and not too much more on other points of sailing.

The best way to judge tune for any given class is to compare yo[u]
boat with the hotshots who win all the races. Take a look at mas[t]
control, jib leads, traveler placement and control, mainsheet rig, and
cut of the sails, among other items. To check tune and the
adjustments to make, it is helpful to work with another boat of the
same class. Use one boat as a constant and run a series of brushes,
making changes in one boat to see whether comparative speed is
improved or hurt. Switch skippers to make sure that one boat isn't
being sailed better. This is not a cut-and-dried method, because of all
the variables, but it can give helpful indications if done long enough
and carefully enough.

Many classes have so many built-in adjustments to rig that the boat
is, in effect, tuned a different way for different conditions and points
of sailing. Items like Barber hauls that adjust the jib leads, and
Cunningham holes at the tack of the mainsail for regulating luff
tension, make instant adjustments possible, so that draft can be
controlled for varying conditions. At one time, to be competitive,
boats had to be equipped with different suits of sails for light and
heavy air and there was always a difficult decision on which suit to
use on a given day, trying to guess ahead of time what the wind
strength would eventually be. Now, with Cunninghams to pl[ay] [wi]th
and other adjustments that can be made during the race, suc[h] [as] [th]e
athwartships position of the mainsheet assembly on the traveler, and
adjustment of the vang, the sail can be flattened for windward work in
moderate breeze or loosened up for a run, or draft can be moved
forward or aft in the sail to suit changes in wind strength. Some
classes do not permit many adjustments, while others provide
unlimited possibilities; it is up to the skipper to become familiar with
what is possible in his own boat.

The boom vang, sometimes called a *kicking strap* or *preventer*, first
came into use as a means of securing the mainsail against a jibe. It
consists of blocks and line in arrangements that vary from class to
class. It is attached to the boom near the forward end of it, and the

other end of the assembly of blocks and line is made fast to the deck or to the base of the mast, again depending on the individual boat. Its tension can be adjusted, and it can be freed and trimmed very quickly, with a jam cleat to set the trim.

From its original purpose of holding the boom so that it can't swing over in an accidental jibe, boom-vang use has been expanded until it is now a major aid to sail trim on all points of sailing. When close-hauled or reaching, it holds the boom down, preventing it from skying up as the sail bellies out, thereby helping the sail to hold its shape. Sails also twist under stress, and the vang helps prevent this action, which gives the lower part of the sail different draft from that of the upper part.

In essence, therefore, tuning is a question of becoming familiar with the potential of one's own boat. Overpreoccupation with it can distract a skipper from the essentials of tactics and strategy and of making the boat go fast on the course, and a good balance between these elements brings the best results.

Getting Ready to Race

Many a race has been lost long before it started, due to failure of skipper and crew to get ready properly. We have already mentioned care of the boat, familiarity with the rules, and tuning. Race-day routine is important, and sloppy organization can ruin all the effort that has gone into getting the boat ready. Starting at home, leave plenty of time to get to the boat, allowing for weekend traffic, drawbridge openings, and other such boobytraps. Have a check-off list of equipment that must be taken from home, and of gear that may be in a locker at the club. It's too late to remember something left in the hall closet when the starting gun is fifteen minutes away.

Check for stopwatch, race circular, tide tables, weather report, foul-weather gear and windbreakers, life jackets, binoculars, sunglasses, sunburn cream, and cold drinks. Before shoving off, make sure of all sails needed, bucket, paddle, cushions, and such obvious boat items as tiller and spinnaker or whisker pole.

Usually there is a last-minute rush for time on the lift or lifts at a club. Everyone can't launch at the same time with five minutes to go. If minor repairs are needed, complete them before race day, or leave extra time. Make sure you have all the right tools and other equipment for doing the job, instead of making a nuisance of yourself trying to borrow from other sailors who are busy with their last-minute chores.

As you rig the boat, check over each part and make sure that it is working properly and that no lines are frayed or pins missing. Allow plenty of time to get out on the course and look over conditions. On the way, check current direction and velocity. Look at the sky for weather indications from the clouds, and check key points on the shoreline, close by and as far away as possible, for indications from flags or smoke of possible changes in wind strength and direction. Look at the other boats to see if anyone is using an unusual sail or trying something different. Study the race circular and check the location of the committee boat and all marks that are visible. Watch the committee boat for signals at all times, but don't ask questions of the committee unless there is some obvious discrepancy. Test your boat on all points of sailing to make sure the sails look right and that everything is working. Don't stray very far from the starting area, but don't interfere with other classes that start earlier.

Starting

If your class is first, check the line closely for favored position, making a few runs at it to see which end is favored without necessarily tipping your hand. Harden up on both port and starboard to see if one is closer to the windward mark. Keep an eye on wind shifts, however, as conditions might change with the next one.

Be sure you know the starting procedure. Most clubs use the

Starts, especially in big fleets, are vitally important

standard routine of the USYRU, in which a white shape goes up with ten minutes to go, signaled by a gun or horn. It is lowered with five minutes thirty seconds to go, and a blue shape goes up at five minutes, with sound signal. The blue shape is lowered with thirty seconds to go, and the start signal is a red shape and sound signal. If for any reason the sound signal fails, the visual signal is the official one and takes precedence. If there is more than one class, normal procedure is to have the start for one class be the five-minute signal for the next one. Some clubs vary this routine with three-minute intervals instead of five, a good idea if there are a lot of classes on a small course, so be sure you know what the system is.

Your crew should be organized, with functions assigned and understood, and chatter should be kept to a minimum. The stopwatch governs the action until the starting gun. Handling it is an important function, and if possible, the crew member who has the job should not have another one. Time should be read off in minutes remaining to the start—"six to go," for example—and need only be done on the minute until the last few minutes, unless the skipper wants a special reading. For the last couple of minutes, fifteen-second intervals should be used, then five-second intervals from the thirty-second warning on, and a countdown by the second from ten-to-go. Except for the stopwatch readings, talk should be confined to pertinent information on wind shifts, actions of other boats, and sail trim. Someone should have the specific job of checking committee boat signals for last-minute changes and to make sure routine is being followed.

If other classes start before yours, watch each one to see if the favored position remains the same or if wind shifts are frequent enough to change it between starts. Don't stray from the starting area, especially in foul tide or light air, and in light air, keep way on your boat at all times. If she is allowed to stop, control is lost and may be hard to reestablish; overcoming inertia and getting the boat going again can be difficult.

Unless very special local conditions prevent it, all races should start with a windward leg, and maneuvers described here are for windward starts. In any start, the key is to have the boat moving well in clear air. If that can be done at the favored spot on the line, it is a perfect start. If being there means that you are fighting every other boat in the fleet for one small patch of water, clear air and boat speed are more important.

To make good starts, you should be familiar with the boat's characteristics as to carry, acceleration, and maneuverability. Tactics differ for boats with varying performance qualities. Light dinghies can sit in one position, luffing and waiting for the gun. As soon as the sheet is trimmed, they will take off at good speed. This is not good practice in heavier boats, however, since a boat with way on will carry past a boat that has been luffing for many seconds after the idling boat

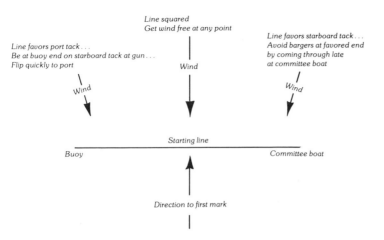

How to analyze and play a starting line

starts to accelerate. In these heavier boats it is important to judge the time needed to hit the line from some distance away with good speed on. Boats with quick turning ability can spin quickly, jibing and tacking at will to find the right opening on the line, while again, heavier boats with bigger turning circles can't make last-minute maneuvers of that type.

If the committee has set up a line that is cocked so badly that one spot on it is highly favored, or if a sudden wind shift brings on this situation in the middle of a starting sequence, starting maneuvers become increasingly difficult. Should the line be cocked so that the windward end is highly favored, serious jams can result at the end. Boats coming in from high on the wind are in the situation known under the rules as *barging,* and they must give way to boats to leeward of them. The leeward boats can head up prior to the starting signal, forcing the bargers up. A boat caught barging is in a helpless position and must tack away and jibe around to stay out of trouble, resulting in a late start. The leeward boats are often helpless, too, with their wind being taken by the jam of boats all trying for the same spot. Exact timing and lots of guts can bring a boat through this kind of start, but it is probably better to try one of two alternatives.

The perils of barging; LE 55 has been squeezed out

Rather than mixing with the jam of boats at the windward end, settle for some distance down the line to leeward as long as your air is clear and the boat is moving. Where you are a few hundred yards after the start is much more important than your spot on the line itself, and the clear air and boat speed could move you well out from the jam of boats interfering with each other.

The other choice is to hang back and purposely start late at the windward end with clear air and a good head of steam. That will give you windward position on all the boats that were tangled there at the gun, and with better boat speed in clear air, you could ride right over them. You will also have control of their ability to tack over onto port, since they probably can't clear you. This late start works particularly well if the wind is continuing to swing right, adding to the advantage of the windward end.

If the line is cocked to favor the other end, a split-second port-tack start that crosses the whole fleet is a great maneuver, but it is difficult to accomplish, especially in fleets of experienced sailors. Just one boat close enough to hold starboard rights ruins the whole procedure and puts the port-tacker in a bad hole. It is usually safer and wiser to run the line on starboard tack so as to be fairly close to the favored end at the gun. If there is room, you can flip to port right away and cross the fleet. If not, you still have a good windward advantage, and your air is clear.

Good starts take practice and experience. They are a matter of good planning plus the ability to make quick improvisations, and it must be admitted that luck often plays a part. The top skippers, however, make good starts too many times in a row for it to be a matter of luck.

The Windward Leg

Windward legs are the key to most races, especially at the club level. In championship competition, all sailors in the entry are so proficient in windward ability that the even more subtle nuances of downwind speed play an important part, but sailors who do consistently well to windward are always in contention, and it is impossible to overcome consistently bad windward work.

As I pointed out in the chapter on basic sailing, the wind is seldom constant in strength or direction, and the object on the windward leg is to use these variations to reduce the angles of the zigzags that must be taken to achieve a spot that is directly to windward. If a boat normally tacks through 90° but—by taking advantage of every shift in wind—can reduce this to 60° or 70°, it is obvious that the distance sailed will be less.

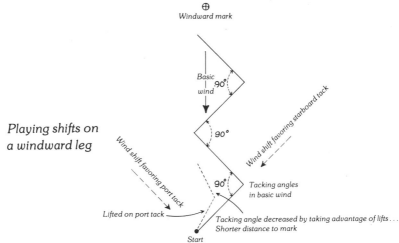

⊕
Windward mark

Basic 90°
wind

90°

Wind shift favoring starboard tack

Playing shifts on
a windward leg

Wind shift favoring port tack

90°

Tacking angles
in basic wind

Lifted on port tack

Tacking angle decreased by taking advantage of lifts . . .
Shorter distance to mark

Start

Increases in wind strength also allow a boat to point higher by increasing the boat speed and bringing the apparent wind forward. A good skipper can detect the approach of lifts and headers, and of stronger puffs, by the look of the water, and by the way the boat reacts. If the boat is being lifted, the telltale will point in toward the sail more, the boat will tend to tip more, and there will be a stronger windward helm. If crew weight reacts to hold the boat flat and not spill the increased wind, and if the boat is allowed to ease up to windward the way she wants to, she will gain windward advantage without slowing down. Everything that brings the boat more to windward reduces the distance to the mark.

If a header hits and the sails start to luff, with the telltale pointing straight aft, the helmsman must head the boat off and keep the sails full. A decision must quickly be made whether to stay in the header and ride it out, if it is a small one, or to tack and turn it into a lift. The tactical situation at the moment often governs this decision, but so far we are discussing pure boat speed and the optimum tacks to take if the boat were alone on the course, racing against the clock.

Wave action also affects boat speed, and a good skipper has to have the feel of his boat in a sea. Playing waves so that the boat isn't fighting the bigger waves, slamming into them and slowing down, is a factor in good helmsmanship. Ease to windward over the smaller waves of a sequence and drive off for best possible speed when the bigger ones hit. It is a question of delicate balance, and a well-sailed boat usually proceeds to windward in a series of controlled, rhythmic *scallops* governed by both wind shifts and wave action. Sailing too close to the wind pinches the boat and slows her down, stalling the sails, and sailing her too wide loses distance to windward and turns the wind force on the sail into more of a heeling action than a driving one.

Boat speed is vital at all times in a race, but it must always be related to the tactical situation of the moment and the overall strategy of the race or series of races. Who is the competition? Which boats matter and which can be ignored? A contest with so many competitors is more complicated than a straight, all-out speed race. The fastest boat doesn't always win sailing championships if she goes to the wrong places or becomes involved with the wrong boats in the fleet. Only in match racing, such as for the America's Cup—with just two boats in competition, like two boxers—is it possible to concentrate completely on one boat. A fleet race is like a gang fight. Just when you are ready to knock out the toughest-looking man in the mêlée, someone catches you from your blind side—lights out.

If you stay in a lift that puts you on one side of the course and your closest competition splits to the other side, how will you be placed when the leg is over?

For those reasons it is important to know, from the standing in the series or regatta, which boats you should be watching, and then to suit your tactics to that decision. *Covering* is vitally important: staying to windward of your competition, keeping between it and the next mark, and tacking on top of it when it tacks so that you stay in the same wind pattern and, ideally, bother the wind supply. If you are trailing and being covered, quick tacks, splitting away just when the other boat has settled on a new tack, can break you free of the cover. One of the most common ways to blow a close race is to fail to cover. Overconfidence over staying in a lift, pure inattention to a split-second tack that must be made to hold a cover, or indecision about which boat to cover when there is a multiple choice in the near vicinity, can be fatal, allowing a trailing boat to break free.

The tacking pattern on a windward leg must be related to the course as well as to the competition. It is a bad mistake to carry on too far on one tack while some distance from the mark, thereby running the chance of *overstanding*, which means that you have gone beyond the point at which the mark can be laid when you are close-hauled. That is all wasted distance and time. At the point at which the mark can be laid close-hauled, with no further tacking, a boat is said to be on the *lay line*. If she then gets a lift and has to free sheets to stay on

It is dangerous to approach mark on port tack, as boat in center is doing

course for the mark, she has again wasted distance. It is important, therefore, to stay inside the lay lines on both sides of the course until arrival in the area near enough to the mark to judge the lay line accurately and to avoid any possibility of overstanding.

It is also advisable to pursue a tacking pattern that will make the starboard tack the final one for approaching the mark. A boat coming in on port tack in a big fleet has to be very lucky to avoid giving way to starboard-tack boats in the approach to the rounding. A great many places can be lost in a close race through being on port tack in this situation.

Nowhere else in a sailing race is it so important to make all the variables come together correctly than on a windward leg. The elements of boat speed must be combined with tactical considerations and the demands of the course. Very seldom can the combination be ignored or varied with success. A prime example of an exception took place in the 1960 Olympics in the Star Class. The sailing Games were held on Italy's Bay of Naples, which has very set patterns of wind behavior in normal weather. Timir Pinegin, the Russian Star entry, arrived three weeks ahead of time and sailed the course area exhaustively every day, building up knowledge of local wind behavior. In the series, he ignored conventional tactics of covering the closest opponents and *playing the fleet*, concentrating instead on playing the wind patterns he had learned in his practice sails. He would go away from the fleet on his own, taking long flyers to an area where experience had taught him the wind would come in first, or shift favorably, and his unorthodox methods paid off with a gold medal.

That is not likely to work in most regattas, where the percentages are seldom with such individualistic maneuvers. Something of an exception can be made, however, in lake sailing in fluky conditions. Often, wind patterns on a lake are completely unpredictable and variable, and two boats might be on opposite tacks and on the same heading within a few yards of each other. In such conditions, the most important consideration is to keep the boat moving well at all times, possibly far off the rhumb line course to the next mark, concentrating on picking up a wind.

The Reaching Leg

Even good sailors tend sometimes to look on the reaching leg of a course as a time to coast and relax, but that is a serious mistake. There are many tricks for increasing boat speed on a reach, and tactical considerations as well. In nonplaning boats, the changes are smaller and less dramatically obvious than in picking up a good lift on a windward leg, but a few inches here and there can mean a tactical advantage on approaching the next mark. In a planing boat, the ability to put the boat on a plane quickly when a puff hits and sustain it as long as possible can bring radical and rapid changes in position. Quick trim of the sails, crew weight hiked out, and the boat steered a bit off the wind are the moves to put a boat on a plane.

If the wind is puffy and variable, the best procedure is to keep high in the lulls, maintaining boat speed and a better apparent wind, then to drive off in the stronger puffs. It is then that a boat can be coaxed on a plane if she has the capacity, and the speed is increased noticeably even in nonplaning boats. Steering should be done gently, without radical rudder moves, since they tend to brake a boat and reduce speed, and the rudder should be used as little as possible, with sail trim taking care of changes in wind direction. The sail should be just on the verge of luffing at all times on a reach. Too-tight trim causes stalling.

Placement of crew weight is as vital on a reach as on any other leg, and the boat should be kept as flat as possible at all times. Fore-and-aft weight placement depends on the characteristics of the boat's design and, very often, on wind strength. The harder it blows, the more important it is to keep weight aft to make the rudder as effective as possible and to prevent the bow from *rooting*. Each class has its doctrine in this situation. In most centerboarders, a minimum of board is all that is needed to aid directional stability without adding wetted surface.

In a big fleet, the whole fleet often tends to go high of the course on a reaching leg as each boat inches up that way to prevent the next boat astern from getting on her wind. That is important, but should this not be a problem, it is usually better to stay a bit low of the course so that the final approach to the mark can be made by hardening up, with a slight increase in speed, rather than having to head off at a slower angle. The strength of the breeze, a puff or a lull, on the approach to the mark, which cannot be predicted, is often the most important governing factor, however.

The late Georg Bruder (BL 3) was an uncanny genius at downwind work; he came from far back to take this lead on a run

It is always important to maneuver for a right-of-way advantage in the upcoming mark rounding, aiming at achieving an inside overlap.

Success on a reach really boils down to getting the most out of a boat's capability for acceleration. If sail trim and steering combine in quick reaction to even the smallest changes, those precious few inches that keep your wind clear and keep you ahead at the mark rounding can be the result.

The Downwind Leg

Again, as in reaching, there is a temptation to let the boat take care of herself on a run and just to go along for the ride, but that type of thinking ignores the many possibilities for improving position on a downwind leg.

To get maximum speed out of the boat, she must be kept in the best possible trim, with the crew weight placed carefully both athwartships and fore-and-aft in a distribution that reduces wetted surface and drag, puts the boat on her best sailing lines, and makes steering easiest. The sail should be out as far as possible, at right angles to the centerline if it is a direct run, and the centerboard should be down only enough for directional stability in centerboarders. Steering should be kept to a minimum to reduce the braking effect of the rudder, and wave action should be used when possible to increase speed. If conditions are such that the boat can be made to surf on the top of breaking waves, those extra bursts of speed can add an advantage. The late Brazilian dinghy expert Georg Bruder had an uncanny ability to play the waves on a run in his Finn dinghy. In Gold Cup competition on the open waters of Lake Ontario, he was able, time and again, to pass boat after boat in an expert fleet by the split-second timing with which he could get his boat surfing and then—by subtle changes in direction at just the right moment, in rhythm with the pattern of the waves—continue the surfing action much longer than any of the boats around him. Naturally that is more important in light-displacement boats with quick acceleration, but the principles apply to any kind of hull, although the results are less immediately dramatic in displacement boats.

Keeping one's wind free is vital on a run, and very difficult to do if boats astern are coming up with fresher puffs. Luffing the nearest competitor up to windward to prevent that one boat from getting by may result in losing several more boats that are able to sail through on a straighter course to leeward. Anticipation of the moves of the boat astern can help, keeping your sail out of the area of another boat's wind shadow before it is too late. Much depends on the direction the next mark is to be rounded, which determines which side will establish right-of-way with an inside overlap. Conversely, an overtaking boat should make every effort to block the wind of the boat ahead and to try to pass on the side that will hold right-of-way at the next mark. Sometimes it pays to hold off and make a move just before reaching the mark so that the overtaken boat has no time to recover and fight back.

The sail should be kept under control at all times, and accidental jibes should naturally be guarded against. If it becomes necessary to jibe to gain an advantage or protect a leading position, it should be done with a controlled jibe, with the sheet rapidly trimmed and slacked to avoid killing boat speed.

In boats equipped with spinnakers, that sail plays the paramount role in effective sailing on reaches and runs. The spinnaker is the most sophisticated sail, requiring more delicate nuances in trim and control than any other sail, and skillful use of it has more to do with downwind success than any other factor.

There are all kinds of spinnakers; larger offshore racers have several of different weights and cuts for varying wind strengths and points of sailing. Different sailmakers have different theories on the best cut for a spinnaker and such methods as *radial cut, star cut,* and *cross cut* (the way the panels of cloth run) have been variously in vogue. In general, spinnakers for downwind work should be full and broad-shouldered, while those for working closer to the wind can be of flatter cut.

Spinnakers can cause trouble if not handled expertly

Spinnakers are controlled by a sheet that leads aft from the unsupported lower corner and a guy that governs trim of the spinnaker pole that is rigged in the mast and holds the other corner of the sail out on the opposite side of the boat from the mainsail. There is also a lift that controls the height of the pole and a foreguy that prevents the pole from skying up. All these except the lift usually lead to the cockpit area, and they must be trimmed in concert as interreacting controls. Normally, the pole should be at right angles to the true wind direction on a run and at a height that keeps both corners of the spinnaker at the same level. In light air, the pole end can be lowered to help the sail stay full, and the sheet can be replaced with a piece of light line. In fresh air, the sail should be high and away from the boat, with the halyard perhaps eased a bit so that the head of the spinnaker should be brought in as close as possible and strapped down hard, "locking" it to the boat to prevent oscillation.

The spinnaker should be trimmed so that the leading edge is just on the curl, not quite luffing, and maintained in that careful balance with constant, delicate trim. A combination of helmsmanship and trimming should be used to keep the sail full and drawing at its maximum efficiency at all times. If a boat is overpowered under spinnaker and starts to tip too much, the boat should be headed off and the sheet freed. The normal tendency to head into the wind to prevent excessive heel is wrong in this case and only increases the heeling moment.

Jibing a spinnaker is a move for experts and when done smoothly can gain tremendous advantages in rounding marks or in close-in maneuvering, where it is important to keep the boat's wind clear. Depending on the boat, there are two ways to effect the jibe. One is by dipping the pole across the foredeck, leaving it attached to the mast at all times; the other is to end-for-end it, switching ends at the mast. The size of the foretriangle governs the method used, because some boats have too long a pole for it to dip across the deck and must use the end-for-end method. In both methods the sail is released from the pole end by tripping a fitting with a controlling line, or the pole is brought forward until a crew member on the foredeck can release the sail from the end of the pole. If the dip method is used, the pole is then swung on through and the opposite corner of the spinnaker is attached to it. What had been the sheet is now the guy; the former guy now acts as the sheet; and the sail is trimmed accordingly. The mainsail should be jibed over at a moment that blankets the spinnaker for the least amount of time. Good coordination of steering and swinging the pole with jibing the mainsail should keep the spinnaker full during the whole procedure. If it collapses and spills air, boat speed is reduced.

In the end-for-end method, the pole end at the mast must be freed from the fitting at the mast. While supported by the lift, the pole is then swung across the foretriangle and the opposite end is attached to the mast fitting while the opposite corner of the sail is being attached to what is now the outer end of the pole. In a hard breeze, this method is more difficult because of having to reseat the pole on the mast fitting.

Those are the bare basics. Spinnaker techniques are worth an exhaustive study and are forever the subject of new discoveries and refinements. The spinnaker is actually an unseaworthy sail for offshore work and therefore requires extra attention and especially strong fittings in long races, such as the 2,300-mile Transpac from Los Angeles to Honolulu. When carefully tended, it pays real dividends in those extra bursts of speed that make the difference in a race.

Rounding Marks

All the good work of a lengthy leg of the course can be wiped out in a few seconds during a mark rounding. That is where the tensest in-fighting occurs and where split seconds and inches make the difference. The rules govern all actions, and it is an absolute must to know them instinctively, since everything happens too fast for anything but instant reactions. The key rule is that governing overlaps. An inside overlap—with the bow of the trailing boat ahead of an imaginary line extending horizontally from the aftermost extension of the leading boat—establishes right-of-way if it has been attained before the leading boat is two boat-lengths from the mark. This is done by hailing—shouting, if you will—and the burden of proof is on the trailing boat to have established the overlap properly.

Once an overlap is established, the outside boat may not deprive the inner one of sufficient room to round the mark properly, which sets up a chain reaction on all boats to the outside of the overlap. That situation has probably accounted for more place changes in racing than any other single situation.

We have already mentioned planning a reaching or running leg to end up on the inside if possible and, in approaching the windward mark, to make the last approach on starboard tack if at all possible. That kind of planning should take place well down the leg, far in advance of the approach to the mark area. We have also mentioned the sin of overstanding. If there is a current, it should be carefully estimated as part of the approach procedure. Many an approach has ended up in an extra tack, a speed-killing pinching action, or a collision with the mark, because of failure to provide for the effect of the current.

In approaching the mark, everything should be in readiness for the next leg. If it is to be a spinnaker run, the pole should be readied on the correct side, and the sail and its controlling lines should also be all set. If it is a leg with a choice of headsails, that too should be settled well in advance. Try to estimate what the wind direction will be on the next leg. If you are to go onto a windward leg, see if you can figure out which tack will be favored after rounding. It is frustrating to stand on into a header after rounding and have the boat astern tack right away and gain rapidly in the lift.

Rudder and sheet trimming should be coordinated in a rounding so that boat speed is not killed by too quick a trim or too radical a move with the rudder. If rounding from a windward leg to a free leg, holding in the sail too long will stall it out and kill speed. Know the turning circle and turning characteristics of your boat so that you sail it through the rounding at full speed without killing speed with too sharp a turn or losing distance with a wide one. That should be practiced many times before starting to race. Maneuverable dinghies can come in close to a mark and make sharp turns onto the new course without hurting speed, while boats with long keels, and displacement boats of all kinds, should be brought in wide in a gently curving arc.

The importance of mark roundings can be seen very graphically when an advantage of a few inches of overlap on the approach can be turned into a lead of several boat-lengths right after the rounding. Competitive sailors love the close-in competition of mark rounding. Sailing isn't a contact sport, but there is the feeling of it here.

Finishing

It is a cliché that the race isn't over until the finish line is crossed, but most closely contested races *are* won and lost in the last few hundred yards. If the lead boat just has one nearby boat to cover and everybody else is out of contention, the problem is simple: stay between your competition and the line. Keep covering right up until the last few yards. The temptation to split off and take a flyer for the line on what looks like a favorable slant can be fatal if the other boat is allowed to go into new, clear air and perhaps get a last-minute lift.

If there is multiple pursuit, the problem is different, and it is probably most important to play lifts and headers on your own, concentrating on boat speed and on aiming for the most favorable spot on the line, in case it is cocked in any way. The complex pattern of a group of boats approaching a finish line on a windward leg in shifty air is one of the most exciting situations in sailing, one that calls for intense concentration and quick improvisation. The worst sin in such a situation is to tighten up and pinch the boat, trying to make the line on one last squeezing tack when it is much more important to keep boat speed up and tack at the right moment. If at all possible, it pays to plan in advance a pattern of tacks that will put you on starboard tack on the final approach, which could control the situation.

Your finish is official when any part of the boat crosses the line. Although it is not necessary to get the whole boat over, it is necessary to clear the finish area without interfering with other boats or recrossing the line without permission.

All this has been a short course in the very long course that covers everything there is to know about sailboat racing. In fact, as we have noted, it is a never-ending course of infinite fascination, built on the basics we have gone through here.

8
Clubs, Committees, and Junior Programs

IN CHAPTER 6 we went over the general framework of sailboat racing and the organizations that govern it. At the local level, there are many administrative details to think about. First of all, most racing is sponsored by private yacht clubs, so something should be known about their organization and operation. There is a growing trend to bypass clubs, as sailing continues to spread in interest and participation; many classes, such as the Hobie Cat catamarans, conduct races out of marinas or off public beaches, with local dealers cooperating in supplying committee equipment and personnel. There are also community clubs, open to all residents of a town or county, which hold racing programs for all comers.

Forming a Club

Most clubs are operated on a membership basis, with candidates for membership proposed by members who know them personally, just like any country club or other form of social club. In some cases, this can be a formalized, snobbish process, but the concept of the "exclusive" club with heavy social overtones is largely outmoded. Some of the old-line clubs in areas where yachting has been carried on since the early days of the sport do conduct their membership process this way, often because there is great pressure, numerically, from those who want to get in. In general, though, active sailing clubs usually welcome sincerely interested sailors.

If there are no club memberships available in an area, and a number of sailors want to band together to form a club so that they can have well-organized racing, there is no reason in the world why they can't do it. The prime movers should call an organization meeting of all who might be interested and, under a volunteer temporary chairman, select a steering committee to follow through with the steps of getting a club started. The meeting can settle on the general purposes of the organization, and perhaps a name. The steering committee then goes about developing a constitution and by-laws, using those of other similar clubs as guidelines. It is probably advisable to have a lawyer get a charter for the organization under the laws of the state. Then a formal organizational meeting under the steering committee completes the ratification and elects a slate of officers, following the most likely example of a table of organization from other clubs. There is no set formula for the exact officers a club should have, and many vary, but a streamlined staff usually makes the organizational tasks easier.

Some clubs get along without permanent facilities, operating out of public parks, marinas, etc., but development of facilities is important when financially possible. Local conditions naturally govern the way they are set up. Items to be considered are: the body of water and its suitability for the type of racing planned; boats to be used (one-designs or a catch-all handicap fleet); storage of boats and equipment and access to water via ramps, lifts, floats, and piers; social functions. Some sort of funding has to be arranged, whether through bonds and initiation fees, bank loans, or some form of subscription among those interested. There are many problems to be solved, but most clubs that are now well established started this way and gradually expanded over the years. No outside affiliation is needed, but a membership in a regional yacht racing association and the United States Yacht Racing Union (see Chapter 6) greatly expands opportunities for competition for the membership.

Race Committee Work

No matter what the sponsorship, sailboat racing needs officiating just as much as football, basketball, or any other sport that must enforce complicated rules in order to have fair competition. As we explained in Chapter 6, it is virtually the only sport where officials can't view all the action, putting a unique enforcement burden on contestants and officials. The pure mechanics of racing must also be administered by a committee: the starting procedure, the establishment of the course, and the recording of the finish.

The big problem lies in finding the right people to serve on the race committee. Inexperienced committee work can ruin the racing, but most experienced sailors want to be out there themselves rather than on the committee boat. Retired sailors who have the knowledge and the time are very often so set in their ways that they are difficult to work with, and they may have lost the physical sharpness needed to run the committee boat well. Eager novices are helpful for subsidiary roles but need supervision and cannot be trusted to set lines and courses correctly.

What to do about the manpower problem? Depending on the size of the club, that can be solved in various ways. For major events such as big open regattas, and class or regional championships, the best sailors in a club who are not involved in the affair as contestants can be given temporary duty so that the club puts on its best possible front. It is the weekly assignment of committee members to keep a club's regular season of races running smoothly that often presents the most difficulties. Should there be a retired racing sailor who has given up competition but still enjoys being afloat and part of the racing scene, and who is still sharp enough to handle the job, the situation is well in hand, and the sailors in the club are lucky. Perhaps their man is not letter-perfect and occasionally sets a barging line or mixes up a starting sequence, but they should grin and bear it and be thankful for his good decisions. Otherwise, they might have to spend at least one day on committee duty themselves, which is another solution.

Rotation of the duty among the experienced sailors is often the best way to staff the committee, especially if different fleets race on different days, and as long as there is an experienced sailor in charge, novices can be used for the rest of the jobs. New members, or parents of youngsters who are coming along in the sport but have no sailing background themselves, are often happy to have this chance to get out on the water and see what is going on, learning something in the process.

With the increasing involvement of women in sailing, more and more of them are becoming accomplished race committee members. Some have the experience to do all the jobs, while others can be used for assistants' jobs, particularly in scoring and recording.

Once the committee is staffed—and this should be the number 1 job of the race committee chairman in setting up a season—its functions must be carefully organized. Details depend on the type of racing and the total conditions, but important generalities apply in all cases. By way of equipment, there should be a committee boat and at least one safety patrol boat. The committee boat cannot be expected to do rescue work and still have the races run correctly. The course should therefore be well patrolled by boats that have safety as their only function. Some system should be set up so that extra boats are available from the club membership on heavy-weather days.

In protected waters, pontoon boats make excellent committee boats, while larger powerboats are needed in open waters. Patrol

Race Committee work is an all-important factor in competition

boats can be whatever is available in the way of small powerboats, but there should be one sturdy open utility for setting out marks and for doing heavy rescue duty. It is easier to do rescue work with inboard boats than with outboards, if there is any choice, since it is handy to have a clear transom for working alongside capsized boats and taking disabled sailboats in tow.

The committee boat should have a signal mast with enough halyards for hoisting signals and shapes, though the white, blue, and red shapes used in the starting sequence can just as easily be flags attached to the end of poles, raised and lowered by hand. A frame for holding course letters is also needed, plus some sort of sound signal. Some committees stick to a signal cannon, but a gun is difficult to operate safely, taking the full attention of one man, while someone with other duties on the committee can easily operate a horn, which is also cheaper, safer, and more reliable.

Course markers vary according to local conditions. Some committees use designated government buoys for turning marks of a course, but that has its drawbacks: the buoys are usually marking a busy channel with heavy traffic that might interfere with the race boats (and vice versa), and they are often favorite anchoring spots for fishermen—another bad source of conflict. It is better for a committee to have its own markers that can be moved at will for precise establishment of proper courses. They should be some form of plastic buoy or float of high-visibility colors, usually orange, with easily handled anchor and line. It is a mistake to put tall poles with marker flags on turning buoys, as they can oscillate too heavily in a chop and foul the sails of boats that are actually rounding them correctly. In a major regatta with long course legs, in which visiting boats are taking part, it is good practice to station, behind the actual mark, a marker boat with a very distinctive flag, balloon, or banner, so that it can be seen at a good distance.

All procedures of the United States Yacht Racing Union should be used as guides in actual running races. Local option can alter some of the provisions, such as changing the time period between signals, but the basic procedures are important. If they are not followed, a club's sailors are at a disadvantage when sailing in other areas where they are in use.

All starts should be to windward if humanly possible. Starting all races from the club pier, no matter what the wind direction, was traditional at many clubs in less sophisticated days, but now sailors everywhere expect a windward start and decent-length first leg to windward as standard procedure. Laying out the course depends on the configuration of the body of water. Where possible, triangular courses with beats, reaches, and runs should be laid out, and the Olympic and Gold Cup courses, which combine triangles and windward leeward legs, are popular in classes where spinnakers are used. At least 50 percent of the race should be to windward, the first leg should be directly to windward, and the starting line should be virtually squared to the wind. If the wind is swinging through constant shifts, the mean direction of the wind should be used for the line. One school of thought believes in cocking a line about 10° in favor of a port-tack start, but that can cause confusion and a poor start if not done properly. If the wind swings more in the direction of port-tack-favored, it will be an unfair line, and squaring to the mean wind is the soundest method. It is particularly bad to set a line that favors starboard tack, which inevitably creates jams at the windward end, with a potential for excessive fouls.

A line should be at least as long as the combined overall lengths of the class that will take up the most room on the line, with a little extra margin for safety. The starting buoy should be passed on the same side as course markers are to be passed, and the committee boat, establishing the other end of the line, is therefore on the outside of the first leg of the course. If possible, courses should be set up so that marks are left to port, to avoid fouls in rounding situations, but a fair windward leg, clear of the shore or shore areas, is a more important consideration than the direction of mark roundings. If several classes are racing on a course with short legs, and there is a possibility that the first starters might have completed the first of several rounds of the course and be back at the starting area before all classes have been sent off, it is a good idea to use separate buoys for starting and turning markers so that the first starters will not interfere with a class still in the starting procedure. Those buoys should be distinctly different in shape or color to avoid confusion in identifying them.

USYRU rules have provisions for changing a windward marker if a wind shift changes the direction of a true beat on the next windward leg while a race is in progress, but that is difficult to accomplish if multiple classes are on a course in all stages of a race. It is advisable, however, if only one class is racing, as long as proper notification can be given with the prescribed signals.

The finish line should be set up directly squared to the last leg of the course and should be as short as practical, to prevent wind shifts from favoring one end too much. The finish buoy should be passed on the same side as in the other roundings during the race, so that the committee boat should again be on the outside of the course, and finishes should be to windward whenever possible. Again, it is advisable to set up a different buoy for the finish line from the turning mark in that area if it is a multiple-class regatta, so that mark rounders and finishers are not in conflict at the same buoy.

In makeup, the committee should have a chairman, one or two people to handle signals, and a recorder or recorders. Functions that must be filled include running the stopwatch; working the visual and sound signals; and sighting the line for premature starters, who must be recalled. If there is manpower enough, there can be one person per function, or they can be doubled up if necessary. The chairman should be in charge at all times and normally should handle the timing. There should be no extraneous chatter, cutting down on the chance for confusion, and the chairman should have a set routine for announcing each step, such as "thirty seconds to white up and gun for Lightnings," "fifteen seconds," and then a countdown of the final ten; the same routine should apply to each signal. At the finish, one person, usually the chairman, should call off sail numbers for the recorder or recorders—perhaps different ones for each class. If it is handicap racing, there should be someone else to call off clock times. (Handicapping methods will be covered in the next chapter.)

Scoring for a series of races is always a subject for differences of opinion. Probably the simplest is a low-point system that gives three quarters of a point for first and then the same number of points as the finish position for the rest of the placings with zero being the figure for the most number of starters in a series, plus one. A high-point system, the reverse of this, also works well, except that the value of first place can't be established until the series is over and the maximum number of starters is known. This system does not work if high points are based on the number in each race, varying with that number. Some classes have specially weighted high-point systems, and a form of percentage system, like a batting average, is also used in some areas. There is a special Olympic scoring system (see table) which puts a premium on finishing well through weighting its scores, but it is not normally recommended for series other than Olympic practice or trial regattas.

The other question in scoring a series is that of the number of drops to allow in recognition of weddings, Cub Scout picnics, vacation trips, and other emergencies. There is no agreed answer to this, but counting about 75 percent of the races is probably a good guideline figure in a club series.

Olympic Scoring System

Seven-race series; six to count. If only six are completed, five are to count, and if five are completed, four are to count. Five must be completed to have a series.

Place	Score
First	0
Second	3.0
Third	5.7
Fourth	8.0
Fifth	10.0
Sixth	11.7

Seventh and thereafter, place plus six; lowest score wins.

Once the boats have completed the course, the race committee's duties are not yet finished. Placings must be figured out and posted as quickly as possible, and someone must be given the responsibility of keeping season standings up to date.

Protests

And then there are protests to be heard. *Protest* is the most unpopular word in the sailing dictionary, yet competition must be run by the rules, fouls must be protested, and hearings on the protest must be held. It is the duty of the race committee to conduct this function in a proper manner so that protests are always kept in the correct perspective. A mistaken philosophy in some sailing circles holds, "Nice guys don't protest," but that way of thinking is very damaging to the sport. Since fouls and infractions usually take place out of sight of the officials, contestants must abide by the rules and by proper protest procedures, or sailing competition becomes pure anarchy and good racing goes out the window.

The people who foster the idea that nice guys don't protest are usually the ones who take the biggest advantage of this way of thinking, getting away with fouls and then, by implication, daring the sailor who has been fouled not to be a nice guy. In the long run, more is gained, and friendships and personal relationships within a club or fleet benefit more, if protesting is done in a matter-of-fact, unemotional way as a matter of course, rather than the system of "Don't protest me this time and I won't do it to you next time." "Owing" a foul to someone else in the fleet creates bad racing and bad situations.

As soon as a foul has been committed, the boat fouled should fly the red protest flag in the proper manner on the starboard shroud, or some spot on that side of the boat if the mast is unstayed, and it should remain up through the race. A protest should never be withdrawn once it can be seen what the outcome of the race will be, as it is not fair to other boats in the fleet who might be affected by the standing of the boat that committed the foul. The fouling boat should be notified as soon as possible that she is being protested, and if her crew admits that the foul was committed, she should then drop out. If she wants a hearing and does not admit to the foul, a counterprotest flag should be flown. That applies when racing under rules in which fouls require complete disqualification. If the 720 rule is in effect, at the option of the race committee, a boat that has committed a foul may make two complete circles before completing the leg of the course on which the foul occurred and then continue racing with no further obligations in connection with the foul. In some fleets, percentage fouls—in which place standings are reduced by a certain percentage, depending on the nature of the foul—are in effect according to class rules or local agreement, but hearings must be held on them in the regular way.

The protesting boat should notify the race committee on finishing that it is protesting such-and-such a boat.

Protests should be submitted to the race committee in writing as soon as possible after the race, and there can be a time limit established by the committee for doing this. The committee should try to hold a hearing as soon as possible, though it may be put off until a later date for mutual convenience.

It is the committee's responsibility to treat protests as routine matters, in no way discouraging them by act or implication, and the hearing should be conducted in an orderly manner. The committee itself may act as a protest committee, or other sailors, who are not involved with the race or class in question, may be designated to hear it. The hearing should be held in private with no unauthorized persons present, and witnesses should be called as needed. Both sides to the protest may hear all testimony. Handling protests with dignity and as a matter of routine is a great help in fostering good competition.

In fact, every action of the race committee is of extreme importance in establishing the quality of a racing program.

Junior Programs

Without a fresh supply of young sailors feeding into the fleets, it is very hard to keep a sailing program continuously healthy. Many clubs owe their strength and vigor to the quality of their junior instruction program. From the age of eight on, most youngsters are ready for formal instruction and able to absorb the basics of sailing. Some are quicker than others, and some never do become interested, but a well-run program has a tremendous number of benefits for clubs and for the children involved. For those who catch on, sailing is one of the earliest means of learning self-sufficiency. A well-run program should also be just plain fun and a highlight of a summer experience.

The specific routines of a program will vary according to the physical set-up of the club, the sailing conditions in the area, the boats available, and the size of the budget, but there are basics that should always apply. There must be boats that can be used, instructions must be organized and professional, and adult supervision by club members is necessary. Young men and women of college age, with perhaps high-school-age youngsters as assistants, consider junior instructor jobs a great way to spend the summer, and there is also a possibility of hiring adult teachers who have the summer off. The only problem with them is a tendency to make sailing instruction seem like regular schoolwork rather than a change from it that is real vacation fun. The schoolroom atmosphere should be avoided.

Lesson fees take care of the instructors' salaries, and it helps if a club can also provide some form of housing if needed, but that depends on the type of community. Boats used for junior instruction inevitably take a beating, and it is usually asking too much to expect owners to let their boats be used, although this may sometimes be necessary when a program is in the early stages of development. It is

Junior programs produce the sailors of tomorrow; Blue Jays are popular junior sailers

much better if the club owns a few boats, with the instructors specifically charged with keeping them in operating condition. Sturdy open dinghies with good cockpit capacity are preferable, to make sure that as many children as possible can be afloat at one time.

Classes should be divided both by age group and by sailing skills, with the instruction program adapted to each group. "Book learning" in knots, seamanship, rules, tactics, and the like should be saved for rainy days as much as possible, with the overall emphasis on activities afloat.

Safety rules should be set up on swimming, use of life jackets, and general conduct. If possible, a parents' committee should cooperate in enforcing these rules, and there should be a duty parent at the club at all times to oversee them and to control behavior and handle emergencies, large or small. Social events like cookouts, picnics, and square dances can add to the fun, too.

Out of such programs, junior racing series on midweek afternoons can be established for various ages and proficiencies, conducted by the instructors just like the regular club series for adults. Team races with neighboring clubs and open junior regattas, bringing many clubs and classes together, all help to spice the summer with excitement and, eventually, to produce a new crop of hot young competitors for the adult fleets.

___9

Handicapping Systems and Level Racing

IF ALL BOATS were created equal, all sailboat racing could be on a boat-for-boat basis, and no one would ever have to worry about measurement rules, handicap systems, and time-allowance tables. Most boats are not alike, however, and ever since sailboat racing was invented, man has been trying to devise ways and means that will handicap different boats fairly enough for them to have meaningful competition.

That is, of course, separate from the one-design principle. We have seen how that works, and it is an important part of sailboat racing. For the type of competitor who likes to look behind him and see who he is beating, who likes to know when he passes a boat that he is really and truly ahead of it, and who likes to realize that he is the winner pure and simple when he crosses the finish line and gets the gun, one-design racing is the answer. It is not free of legal hassles and technicalities, for there are always arguments about just what the rules and specifications of a class really mean. Someone is always trying to fudge a bit on the standards set by a class—which is, in effect, denying the spirit of one-design racing—but that sort of rumpus pales in comparison to the emotional upheavals caused by the handicapping systems that are used in an attempt to equalize boats of different sizes, specifications, and characteristics.

It is obvious that some system is necessary if thirty-five-footers and seventy-footers are to compete with each other in an ocean race to Bermuda, for example, and virtually all ocean racing is on a handicap basis. Shorter races around the buoys for auxiliaries of different sizes must also be on a handicap basis, and some clubs, especially when they are just getting started and have a fleet of miscellaneous boats in competition, pit small one-designs of different classes against each other in a single fleet and need some system of handicapping them, too.

Handicap racing has been with us since the first formal event of the Royal Yacht Squadron at Cowes, and I think it is safe to say that there has never been a system absolutely satisfactory to everyone and there never will be one. Loopholes, inequities, and misapplications always seem to crop up no matter how carefully a handicapping system is figured out, and the more intense competition has become in recent years, the more pressure there has been on the rules and formulas. Agitation for change and "improvement" never ceases, and the cries of owners whose boats have been left behind competitively through a change in the rules are as anguished as ever, or more so.

On the face of it, it would seem simple enough to devise a formula that would be foolproof in assigning handicaps to sailboats, but that has never been the case. We have seen that sailing is a matter of infinite variables in the way wind, weather, waves, boat design, crew skill, condition of equipment, cut of sails, and just plain luck combine to bring success. Most of these factors can never be formalized in a rule. The emphasis therefore has always been on design factors, which can almost be measurable. A formula can be devised that will nearly equalize design factors under a given set of conditions,

Handicapping permits racing for a diversified fleet like this

but—since conditions seldom remain uniform for the length of a short race, much less one of hundreds of miles across open water—all that equalization can be wiped out by a wind shift or change in wind strength. It is because of this infinity of variables that handicap racing can never guarantee equitable results at all times, but it is still an extremely important part of the sailboat racing world.

How is handicapping applied? First, a boat must be given a rating, based on some sort of measurement formula, and then some system must be devised for applying this rating to race results. The rating is a number arrived at as the result of a formula that balances various elements that affect a boat's speed potential. The elements of the formula are put into equation; the single number that results from this equation is the boat's rating.

There are two ways of relating this rating number to the results of a race. A time allowance based on the rating can be applied against the distance of the race, or against the time consumed in finishing the race. The first method is called *time-on-distance,* and the second is known as *time-on-time.* In general, the former has been used in North America, and the latter in British and European events.

In the time-on-distance method, a table of allowances is used to apply rating to distance. Every rating number is given an allowance in seconds per mile. For example, if a boat that rates 15 is allowed fifty seconds per mile over a theoretical or actual scratch boat at the top of the rating list, and another boat that rates 20 is allowed forty seconds per mile (those figures are selected purely for use as an example and are not based on any existing formula), the smaller boat gets an allowance of ten seconds per mile over the bigger one. In a six-mile race, the smaller boat could finish up to a minute behind the larger boat and still beat it on corrected time.

The actual table of allowances in use in races sanctioned by the United States Yacht Racing Union has been worked out by computer under the assumption that there will be a certain percentage of windward work, reaching, and running in a given race, a development of a table first worked out step by step by Nathanael Herreshoff in the 1860s. If an ocean race happens to be sailed under conditions that produce just one point of sailing for the entire course, the table of allowances no longer provides an equitable basis for working out corrected time, an inherent weakness in the system that brings about a situation in which certain conditions are "big boat" and others strongly favor small boats. In some races in which it is known that there will be all downwind work because of prevailing breezes, race committees sometimes put a correction factor into the table of allowances ahead of time, but that is done only rarely.

Since time-on-distance produces a figure that can be worked out in advance of a race, the time allowance between boats is the same over that distance whether the race is a very fast one or a drifter. You know in advance that Boat A gives you so many minutes' handicap, and that's the way it remains.

In time-on-time, the allowance is a percentage. The longer a race continues, the larger the time gap will be between boats. There is no knowing just how much difference there will be in the corrected times of boats until the race is over. This system probably has even more inequities than time-on-distance, and both methods have their proponents and opponents.

The single most important figure in determining a boat's speed potential is its waterline length, which theoretically puts a top limit on what a boat is capable of achieving, and the simplest rating formula would be to handicap a boat on waterline length alone. Very often, after having been worked through the book-length formulas that have been evolved in modern ocean racing, taking in all sorts of arcane measurements and provisions, a boat's rating will still come out fairly near the waterline length.

The next most important measurement is sail area, and a simple formula based on waterline length and sail area can provide quite a fair basis for rating a group of boats casually gathered for a race. That type of rule was used in the early days of sailing, and it sufficed as long as boats were not built specifically to beat the rule. When they were, it became very easy for smart designers, such as Nat Herreshoff, to develop *rule-beaters*, boats that could make a mockery of such a simple formula by the length of their overhangs and the way the overhangs became part of the waterline length when the boat heeled slightly to her sailing lines. More sail area could be crowded on the longer hulls, and soon something had to be done to penalize these advantages. Rules therefore became more complicated, calling for more points of measurement and sail area penalties, and the ball started rolling toward the tremendously involved formulas that are used in arriving at modern measurement rules.

Clubs conducting racing for a mixed fleet of boats can still use a variation of the old waterline-sail area rule that works quite well as long as the boats were not built to beat it. *Yachting* magazine developed such a formula for use in its One-of-a-Kind Regattas, which it sponsors every few years to test various one-design classes against each other. It works well for boats of basically similar type, but such disparate types as displacement keel boats, planing centerboarders, and multihulls should be raced in separate groups to achieve any real fairness.

The formula is:

$$\text{Rating} = \frac{L + 1.3\sqrt{\text{sail area}}}{2}$$

in which $L = \dfrac{\text{length overall} + .7\,(\text{waterline length})}{2}$

Special allowances can also be added for lack of spinnakers, and arbitrary performance factors can also be included, based on local experience. In measuring sail area, the spinnaker is not included, and the foretriangle is the area of the largest jib, or 130 percent of the foretriangle area, whichever is smaller. The foretriangle is measured from the jib hoist to the tack to the mast at the deck, or at tack level in deckless boats. Waterline length is best measured with crew aboard and in normal position, although design figures can be used if there is no opportunity for actual measurement.

Another method for handicapping small boats of different classes is

The One-of-a-Kind formula works well for boats of a similar type

called the Portsmouth Yardstick, named for the English sailing center where it was first developed. This system uses a published list of Portsmouth Numbers for all well-known classes, assigned from known performance factors, and the Number is used as a rating for figuring corrected time. The USYRU has a publication giving full information on use of the Portsmouth Yardstick.

Clubs sponsoring handicap racing for cruising auxiliaries cannot use the Portsmouth system, as it is only worked up for one-design classes. They can use a simplified formula such as the *Yachting* One-of-a-Kind, or perhaps a slightly more sophisticated one such as that sponsored by the Off Soundings Club of Connecticut (as long as no one builds specifically to beat these rules).

Many clubs or area associations have developed a version of the Portsmouth system known as Performance Handicap Ratings. In those, a committee establishes arbitrary ratings for boats based originally on their measurements and characteristics, and then alters the rating if actual racing proves it inequitable. Sometimes the record of individual skippers is worked into a rating as well. That method is becoming increasingly popular, and it does allow racing between boats of widely varying size and characteristics without expensive measuring and computerized ratings.

That form of rule has come into use in reaction to the increased complexity of the rules that have been developed for rating boats in major competitions. For many years there were two major rules for offshore events: the Cruising Club of America Rule in North America, and the Royal Ocean Racing Club Rule in England and throughout much of the rest of the world. Over the years, those rules grew apart in basic provisions until it became increasingly difficult to conduct good international competition. Boats rating well under one of the rules seldom did well under the other one, and an English boat was at a disadvantage in the Bermuda Race, while an American one had the same problem in the Fastnet Race, for example.

An agreement was worked out in the late sixties in an effort to foster better international competition, and the International Offshore Rule was devised for worldwide use. Instead of settling differences and arguments, however, it tended to outmode many of the top boats under the two former rules. A breed of boat rapidly developed that was a specialized racing machine, ruining the old concept that an ocean racing boat was a combination cruiser-racer. The IOR was also changed several times, quickly outmoding the first boats built under it, and many clubs sponsoring handicap racing veered away from using it, developing their own performance rules or reverting to simplified versions of the older rules. The question of how to rate and handicap boats for fair racing will remain controversial as long as there is competition. The basic split concerns whether a rule is a building rule, encouraging designers to come up with new concepts under its provisions, or simply a handicapping rule, a vehicle to provide time allowances for existing boats without affecting their characteristics. "You pays your money and you takes your choice." Speaking of money, the expense of the trends encouraged by the IOR was another reason for the turning away from it after half a dozen years of trial and error.

Under the concept that a measurement rule is a building rule, not a vehicle for working out time allowances, a form of racing that has existed in some way for many years has recently become increasingly popular for topnotch competition under the term *level racing.* In level racing, boats are individually designed and may have widely varying characteristics, but their rating must be the same. They then race on a boat-for-boat basis, like a one-design fleet, with no time allowances.

This is not a new concept, although the term is a new one. In years past, under such rules as the Universal Rule and the International Rule, boats were built to certain formulas for boat-for-boat racing, with individual design characteristics a very important factor. Best known were the Meter classes, including the 12-Meter Class used in America's Cup competition since 1958. Although the 12-Meter Rule has fairly stringent provisions, and it would be impossible to build a planing boat or some other radical type to it, it does allow designers individual play in balancing the elements of the formula as well as in working out the hull lines. There is no one measurement on the boat that is 12 meters, but the formula balancing waterline length, sail area, displacement, ballast, and the figures at certain specified measurement points, along with some limiting provisions on rig and specifications, must form an equation whose answer is 12 meters. Two 12-Meter yachts that measure under the rule and race each other boat-for-boat could rate quite differently under CCA or IOR measurements, and one would have to give the other a time allowance. Other Meter classes have included 5.5-, 6-, 8-, and 10-Meters; they were premium classes for many years until they became too expensive because of quick obsolescence. They were all used for day racing in their own major competitions but were sometimes converted to distance racing by the installation of accommodations.

Distance racing did not have this form of competition, though there were one-design classes that could race against each other boat-for-boat and also engage in handicap racing against all others. The New York Yacht Club 32s, developed in the 1930s, were an example of this, and later such stock boats as the Cal-40, Columbia 50, and Concordia carried on the concept.

Modern level racing developed out of the oddly named One Ton Cup competition. Just as there is no measurement of 12 meters on a 12-Meter, so has One Ton nothing to do with the size or weight of the boats in that category. The One Ton Cup dates back to the late nineteenth century in France, when it was raced for by boats of that measurement designation. It was retired and unheard of for many years, but was then revived in the 1960s for international boat-for-boat racing for yachts rating the same under the RORC Rule. The concept caught on quickly, helped by the fact that boats from many different countries won the early regattas, and the competition soon developed into one of the most expertly sailed and hotly

"Robin," a One Tonner, is a typical level racing boat

contested in the sport. Top designers vied in turning out new designs, and some of the world's keenest sailors became involved in the regattas. When the IOR came in, the One Ton rating was established at 27.5, meaning boats roughly in the thirty-five-to-forty-foot size range, and the usual One Ton Regatta included several one-day round-the-buoys races of about thirty miles, a middle distance race, and a long race of two hundred to three hundred miles. Competition was so fierce, and techniques and expertise were so finely honed, that the "Ton Boats," as they came to be called, became the hottest ones and biggest threats when they engaged in open competition in such events as the Southern Ocean Racing Conference and the Bermuda Race, beating larger boats on a boat-for-boat basis and taking many of the prizes.

The idea spread to other sizes, to categories known as Quarter Ton, Half Ton, Three-Quarter Ton and Two Ton, none of which have anything to do with those weights—they just use the designation as comparisons to the One Tonners—and they too developed topnotch competitors within their ranks.

Level racing has raised the standard of competition and produced some of the stars of the sport, but it has not become numerically significant because of the same old problem of quick obsolescence. This year's Ton champion is next year's party boat, so hot and heavy has the competition been in design and in development of gear and techniques. For those with Grand Prix aspirations, it is the most exciting kind of racing, combining the head-to-head tensions of one-design action with the challenge of developing a boat as a very special racing machine, and you know you're the winner when you hear that gun, a satisfaction denied to those who race under handicaps for corrected-time finishes.

_10

⊙istance Racing

ON THE improbable date of December 11, off Sandy Hook at the entrance to New York Harbor, in the year 1866, the type of sailing competition known as *ocean racing*—or more properly, *distance racing,* since it is popular on the Great Lakes—came into being. From that date, when the schooners *Henrietta, Fleetwing,* and *Vesta* staged their money match with professional crews manning them and sixty thousand dollars in owners' bets riding on the outcome, there

"Henrietta" won the first ocean race in 1866

was a tradition to follow, although the differences between that rugged winter race and today's events would have to be measured in light-years.

About the only similarity remaining is that it takes a great deal of money to campaign an ocean racer. Today the crews are all amateur, money prizes are not the object, and no one would dream of setting out to race across the North Atlantic in December. The 1866 event came about as the result of a whim. Three wealthy New Yorkers, arguing in the bar of an exclusive club about who had the fastest schooner, decided on less-than-sober impulse to settle the question by having their professional crews race the boats to England.

Until then, distance racing had been confined to the deadly serious "races" in which commercial ships vied for the rewards in cash that would come to a vessel making the fastest passage for such money routes as New York to San Francisco or Hong Kong to London.

Today's ocean racing is highly organized, growing all the time in number of entries, and governed by complex handicapping, as we have seen in the previous chapter. Actually, the sport did not really catch on until the twentieth century. The loss of six crew members from *Fleetwing* when her cockpit was swept by a breaking sea, still the greatest lost of life in ocean racing, perhaps put a damper on enthusiasm for racing across oceans, and the only other nineteenth-century events were a few match races for wagers between rich owners. In 1898, members of Chicago YC staged a race to Mackinac Island, 333 miles away at the head of Lake Michigan, to settle another barroom argument, which makes this event the oldest regularly scheduled distance race, as well as the longest one on fresh water. Since it is held annually, it has also been held more often than any other race, many of which are biennial.

Other milestones in the history of ocean racing were the Transatlantic Race for the Kaiser's Cup in 1905, and the first Bermuda and Honolulu Races in 1906. The latter has been run biennially since then, with a 1912-1923 hiatus, and the Bermuda

Race also lapsed, after a couple of lightly attended attempts to keep it going, until a revival in 1923. It was a great success then and since 1924 has been run biennially with the exception of 1940, 1942, and 1944, developing into the premier event in the sport.

The Kaiser's Cup race was notable for two things. Most important from a sailing point of view, the great 185-foot schooner *Atlantic* set a record for transatlantic sailboat racing that still stands: twelve days, four hours, one minute, and nineteen seconds from Sandy Hook to the Lizard, including a phenomenal day's run of 341 miles. The other memorable aspect of the race is that the "solid gold" trophy donated by Germany's Kaiser Wilhelm turned out to be thinly plated and became a propaganda weapon in World War I when the fact was discovered through the cup's being presented for melting down to help the war effort.

While these distance events were attracting attention, shorter races in coastal waters also began to dot the calendar, and average yachtsmen, as opposed to the wealthy absentee owners who had professionals race their boats, began to become involved. World War I called a halt to all activity, but the sport was renewed with added enthusiasm in the 1920s, given a big push by the Bermuda Race revival. A watershed event was another transatlantic race, this time to Spain in 1928, with *Atlantic* once more a participant. Wilson Marshall had been her owner in 1905, and she was now owned by Gerald Lambert.

She did not get the conditions that sent her charging across in a welter of foam in 1905, and it was considered highly significant that the race was won by a "small" boat with an amateur crew, the sixty-two-foot schooner *Nina*. The race was sailed in two divisions, with the small boats sent off a week ahead as their time allowance. *Nina* startled the sailing world and the holiday crowds at the finish at Santander by being the first to arrive. The King of Spain, an ardent sailor who had donated the cup for the race, was so excited that he jumped to the cabin top of the royal launch when greeting *Nina* at the finish, waved his cap, and shouted, "Well done, *Nina*. I am the King of Spain!"

This event was a milestone for several reasons. First, it was the end of the era of the grand yachts, professionally crewed. The crew of the big schooner *Elena* had struck for higher wages before the race, and never again were ocean racers crewed predominantly by professionals. *Nina's* startling win, in which an amateur crew worked her to windward like a big dinghy in the light going near the finish, followed by the stock-market crash the next year, dramatized the changes that were to take place in the near future. The Bermuda Race, with predominantly amateur crews in the boats, also did much to demonstrate that yachtsmen—previously thought of as white-flanneled afterguard types who sipped champagne in the lounge while the paid hands, including the skipper, did the work—could handle sailing vessels well in rugged offshore conditions. After 1928, distance racing belonged to the amateurs. They don't start races in northern latitudes on December 11, and the cliché for characterizing the sport is that it can be compared to sitting under a cold shower while tearing up large-denomination bills and shoving them down the drain. But the natural challenge of it holds a true fascination for those who find a lack of such challenges in the normal patterns of modern living. Many a sailor has stepped ashore after a rugged race crying, "Never again!" at the top of his voice, but he is usually back for the next one. The most oft-heard phrase during the miseries of a cold, wet midwatch is "What the hell are we doing here?" But the fascination, however perverse, persists, and the ocean racing sailor is one of the true fanatics of the sporting world.

Nina is particularly significant in the whole history of distance racing. Through racing *Atlantic,* she is linked with the true beginnings of the sport in the twentieth century, and she carried on as a dominant vessel in it until 1966, remaining highly competitive right into the age of Dacron, fiberglass, and the onset of the IOR. She probably won as many trophies in her thirty-eight years of top-level competition as any yacht ever has, climaxed by victory in the 1962 Bermuda Race, and she is the outstanding representative of an era in which a well-built, well-designed, well-maintained boat could remain competitive for a

Commodore DeCoursey Fales kept "Nina" competitive for many years beyond her normal time

great many years. She also illustrated another trend by gradually changing characterization from a "small" boat to a "big" one. Not many matched her phenomenal span of success, but she personified the era in which good campaigners carried on year after year. The death at age seventy-eight of her owner, DeCoursey Fales, who had rescued her from an early trip to the boneyard in 1935, then restored her lovingly and raced her as hard as any boat has ever been campaigned, while his regular crew was sailing her without him in the 1966 Bermuda Race marked the end of her career as a major ocean racer, but that would have come anyway in the next year or two with the onset of the IOR. From the twenties to the late sixties was one era in distance racing. It has been a very different sport since then.

The first major trend of the twenties was the dominance of the fishing schooner type, with John Alden leading the way with his *Malabar*s. When the Bermuda Race was revived in 1923 and quickly achieved stature as a major event, husky schooners that were adaptations of the commercial fishing vessels were the most suitable yachts then in being for taking offshore for a race or a cruise. John Alden himself was a genius at sailing them, and his victories in 1923, 1926, and 1930 with *Malabars IV, VII,* and *X* put him at the top of the heap, a dominant influence. As the races continued to attract attention, and transatlantic racing also came back in vogue, new thinking also emerged. A young designer named Olin Stephens turned out the fifty-two-foot yawl *Dorade*, with his father's backing, for the 1930 transatlantic race, and she represented a radical departure from the husky Alden fishermen. Slender, long-ended, and with a modern, high-aspect Marconi yawl rig, she was a dramatic contrast, and she startled the sailing world with a smashing victory in the race to England that year. The event attracted enough attention to merit Stephens and his brother Rod, a seamanship and rigging expert, a ticker-tape parade up Broadway on their return, the only time this honor has been accorded yachtsmen.

The Stephens era continued in the thirties with such designs as *Stormy Weather*, winner of the 1936 transatlantic race, and *Edlu*, Stephens's first Bermuda winner in 1934, both developments of the *Dorade* school. Alden and the other designers, such as Phil Rhodes, began turning out boats of this type, and the typical ocean racer, by the World War II break, was a far more sophisticated vessel than the bluff fishing schooners of the twenties.

The postwar years saw a consolidation of these trends, as fleets began to grow, and interest in the sport spread to more and more areas. It had started as an Amerian sport, but the British established their premier event, the Fastnet Race, soon after the Bermuda Race revival, and there was worldwide interest and activity by the 1940s. In addition to the two biggest United States races, the Bermuda and Honolulu (also known as the Transpac), the series of winter races in southern waters known as the Southern Ocean Racing Conference grew to major status. The races from Chicago and Port Huron to Mackinac each summer, various West Coast races to Mexican ports, the Annapolis-Newport Race, the Halifax Race, the Swiftsure in the Pacific Northwest, and sporadic transatlantic races continuously attracted larger and larger fleets. Bermuda Race participants went from 46 through 89, 111, and 135 to the 170s; the Mackinacs went up to several hundred boats; and a West Coast catch-all overnight race from

John Alden's "Malabar X," the ultimate in the fisherman-type offshore racer, was 1930 Bermuda winner

"Highland Light," Bermuda course record-setter in 1932, marked a transition from the fisherman types

Newport Beach to Ensenada, Mexico, attracts fleets of more than 600 on a regular basis.

In that era, the boats continued to be thought of as cruiser-racers. Once an owner had a boat that suited him and brought him some measure of success, he kept her for a period of time, perhaps not as long as *Nina's* career under Fales, but long enough to fit her out to his own requirements in every respect for cruising comfort as well as racing, and to be familiar with her sail inventory, gear, and special characteristics. Year after year boats like *Nina, Stormy Weather, Ticonderoga, Finisterre,* and *Escapade* appeared in major events and were yardstick boats for measuring the performance of newcomers. It was normal to use them extensively for cruising as well and there was nothing incompatible about the two functions. Most of them were custom-built and custom-designed.

Carleton Mitchell's "Finisterre" was the dominant ocean racer of the late fifties

The first break from this tradition came with the success of stock fiberglass boats in the mid-sixties. A stock boat like a Cal-40 could be bought for a third to a half of the cost of custom boats of similar size and began to whomp them thoroughly on the racing course. The Cal-40, designed by William Lapworth, became the single most successful stock design in ocean racing history, scoring victories in the SORC, in the Bermuda Race, and repeatedly in the Transpac, as well as in many lesser events. This trend brought many newcomers into the sport, expanding fleets rapidly and taking the design play away from the few long-run experts, opening up the field to new, younger designers working with stock-boat manufacturers. The Cal-40s also marked a trend to light-displacement boats with fin keels and separate rudders, a distinct change from the deep, wineglass hulls and longer keels of the conventional boats of the era. What was lost in comfort and seakindliness was made up for in surfing ability off the wind, and a greater preoccupation with weight was an indication that the dual cruiser-racer function would be harder to maintain. The advent of the IOR, as described in the previous chapter, and the subsequent de-

The Cal-40 led a stock boat revolution in the sixties

velopment of level racing boats as the hottest types in open fleet racing too, brought about the biggest and most rapid change of all in the history of ocean racing. As the Ton boats were refined to extremely efficient and successful racing machines, with all weight concentrated amidships and the cabin interiors set up for the barest functional necessities, the boat with full cruising amenities, enclosed heads, powerful engine, paneling, regular bunks, and complete galleys could no longer be competitive.

Even the new IOR boats became obsolete very quickly, with the competitive life of one in the so-called Grand Prix events virtually limited to one season, as designers found new ways to build to the IOR. Increasingly events were sailed in divisions, with the IOR boats in a separate class, and Performance Handicap, cruising canvas, Off Soundings, and other categories used to fill out the entry list. The Cruising Club of America, under whose rule the Bermuda Race had been competed for through the 1960s, tried the IOR Mark III for two races and then decided to amend the IOR with new provisions for the 1976 race in an attempt to give a better break to older boats that had not been designed under the IOR.

The argument over the best rule for ocean racing continues and will probably never cease. Someone will always find ways to design boats faster under whatever rule is in effect, making obsolete last year's hotshots, and there will always be attempts to plug the loopholes. It is inherent in the sport.

Aside from the rule question, the techniques and strategy of distance racing are quite different from one-design and buoys racing, although more and more boats, with the increased popularity of level racing, are being staffed by crews with small-boat backgrounds. Distance racers have always known that a boat has to be driven hard continuously, with no let-up, to win, but the type of concentration that goes into an afternoon race was not found very often until the great explosion of interest in the sixties. It takes a dedicated crew, with great stamina and perfect organization, to apply dinghy-racing techniques continuously to a race of several days' duration.

It is especially hard when, as can often happen, no other competitors are in sight. It is one thing to trim and steer as carefully as possible with the rest of the fleet surging all around you, but it is something else to keep up the same intensity of effort alone at night on a dark sea. Distance racing is really a race against time, with the knowledge that the clock is ticking your time allowance away as the only spur to constant effort. Even boat-for-boat action is different. If yachts of different size or rating happen to be in the same water, one of them can waste time worrying about the other boat instead of aiming at a faster finish. The one-design technique of covering can be a mistake, holding a bigger boat back, and it is not uncommon for a smaller boat that is going well to come apart under the pressure of being passed by a larger boat that should be going faster anyway. A nervous skipper will sometimes change sails unnecessarily or lose his concentration under such a circumstance.

Navigation is naturally extremely important in distance racing. If you don't know where you are, it's hard to sail the best possible course. In some races, electronic instruments are allowed, such as Omni, Loran, and even radar, while others place restrictions enough so that old-fashioned celestial navigation is necessary. In any event, despite the presence of all sorts of electronic aids, the navigator in an offshore race should also be able to do celestial, since a power failure, shutting down all instruments, could be disastrous. In the Bermuda Race, the behavior of the Gulf Stream is a vital factor in how the boats fare in crossing it. Usually advance information is given on the general direction and strength of the Stream and on any *meanders:* variations in direction from the general southwest-northeast route of the main body of the Stream. Those can be observed by aircraft and plotted with some accuracy for a few days at a time, and the navigator who finds a favorable meander accurately can be the hero of the race. In most races, knowledge of whatever currents there are is extremely important, and they must be figured into race strategy.

Familiarity with the vessel, and with what sail combinations go best in certain conditions, is another important aspect of distance racing. Since there is often no other boat nearby as a measuring stick of "How are we doing?" the right choice of sails is a matter of the skipper's knowledge of his boat and of what she will do. It is a common error to lug too much sail under the impression that this will keep up her speed. Actually, it is just as important to know when to reduce sail as to add the right sail at the right time. Lugging excess sail overpowers a boat and makes her harder to steer, which slows her down.

That is not new. If anybody was ever familiar with his own boats and knew what they could do, it was John Alden. Expert sailors who crewed for him in offshore races were always amazed at the way he could get an extra fraction of a knot out of a boat when they were sure that everything was just right. The watch on deck would have a sail combination and state of trim that pleased them and seemed perfect, when Alden would poke his head up the hatch and take a look around. Without saying anything, he would walk around to the many lines a schooner has to trim her sails, slack one an inch or two, take up the same amount on another, raise the peak of a gaff just so, and—in extreme cases—perhaps change from one size to another. The boat, which had seemed to be going beautifully, would step up her pace and take off.

When to reduce sail, though perhaps not as far as "Windward Passage" has here, is important in distance racing

Knowledge of that stripe is only gained through long experience, and the owner who doesn't have that touch himself can still do well by organizing a crew that has the experience. Many a winning owner, who accepts the trophy at the end of a race with a wide grin, has been made by his sailing master, a veteran sailor who can call the shots on sail selection and trim. Very often, that person will be a sailmaker, and sailmakers are much in demand on ocean racers.

The navigator and sailing master are important, but a good crew must be organized well through the whole list. There is no room for "passengers" on most ocean racers, unless it is the owner who foots the bill, and the crew should be a good mix of afterguard types, who make the strategic decisions and run the watches, and "deck apes" who man the foredeck for sail changes, grind the winches, and provide the muscle for the constant alterations in trim that should never cease if a boat is to keep going at her top potential.

All these elements, important as they are, can be wasted if the boat is not "steered fast." Helmsmanship is vitally important. Carleton Mitchell, one of the most successful ocean racing skippers of all time with his three Bermuda Race wins in *Finisterre,* plus SORC wins and other top trophies, admitted much of his success came from advance planning of every detail, with crew organization and makeup of paramount importance. He collected the best helmsmen he could find and allowed no one who was not a proven helmsman of top skill to take the wheel. "What's the use of spending money for the best equipment possible to get a few extra seconds per mile of speed and then throw it away with bad helmsmanship?" was the way he put it in perspective.

In some boats, everyone on watch shares helm duties in a timed rotation by the half hour or hour, no matter how they rate as a fast steerer—an inefficient system unless everyone on board is equally good at the wheel. The top boats usually have a few designated helmsmen, and they share the duties by time rotation, or by their own subjective reaction to how they are doing. *Noryema* won the 1972 Bermuda Race with just two helmsmen, who spelled each other as they saw fit, judging their own reactions. This system is a bit extreme and hard on the morale of the rest of the crew, especially if there are long periods with no sail changes or other action, and the crew just sits on the rail and gets wet. If a crewman is capable of steering well, he should be given a turn on the wheel as a morale-booster if nothing else.

All these functions must be blended in a workable watch system if a race lasts more than a few hours. Even on an overnight race, a crew's efficiency drops if no one gets any rest. Some young, tough crews can drive a boat continuously, with no real break for sleep or changing of the watch, for twenty-four hours or so, but they are exceptions. If a crew does not pace itself and pushes too hard without a break, efficiency can drop just at the key point of the race: the approach to the finish. A watch system should be devised so that the boat is always being driven to her maximum by a fresh portion of the crew. There are always a few all-hands situations, where the watch below is routed out to make a major sail change or do some quick spinnaker jibing, but offwatch sleep is an important ingredient in crew efficiency.

There are several ways to rotate the watches. If the race is not too long, say overnight or a couple of days, a straight four-on-four-off rotation works well enough, but that is not a good idea for a long race. One watch always gets the midwatch—midnight to 4:00 A.M. or however the times break—which is definitely a morale factor, and many experienced skippers prefer a system that has different-length watches at different times of day. Some method of *dogging* the watch, breaking up the steady routine of four-on-four-off, is advisable. Splitting the late-afternoon watch into two two-hour watches is one method of changing the rotation, but many experienced skippers prefer a system that has three four-hour night watches and two six-hour day watches, or four three-hour night watches and two six-hour ones during the day.

The skipper might not stand any watch if he has two good watch captains and a big enough crew, or he may take one watch and his top-ranked assistant the other. If possible, the navigator should not be a watch-stander on long races, though it can vary with the size of the crew and the amount of work he must do. Cooking must also be provided for, and that too is a vital function. Some crews can tough it through an overnight race on saltines, sandwiches, and raw fruit, but again, a crew's efficiency drops in long races if the chow is poor and irregular. A good sea cook is invaluable. Without one, the chore must be divided up, and one system is to have the watch coming on duty prepare a meal and the watch coming off do the cleaning up.

Great thought should be given to the type of food and the ease and efficiency of serving it. In rough weather, a one-dish stew or hot soups and drinks may be the only thing possible, and then the hand-held items like crackers, cookies, fruit, raw vegetables, hard-boiled eggs, and even candy save the day—and the midwatch. Supplies of this sort should be part of the planning. With the preoccupation with weight in modern ocean racers, especially the smaller ones in the One Ton range, choice of food, stowage, and preparation become a particularly tricky problem.

Personal gear is also important, especially with the emphasis on saving weight. It goes without saying that it should be kept to a minimum and carried in a collapsible duffle or sea bag. Anyone who boards an ocean racer carrying a hard suitcase either will be told right away what a mistake he has made or will never be asked back. The climate and local conditions govern the type of clothing, though it is surprising how cool a night watch can be anywhere at sea. Many a sailor on the SORC has shivered through the night hours because he thought it never got cold down south. Good foul-weather gear and nonskid knee boots are Number 1 on the list. The foul-weather clothing should be tough and sturdy but light in weight and flexible, allowing freedom of motion for deck work. Sweaters and windbreakers are important, as are tough, comfortable pants. In cold climates wool near the body is great for warmth, and thermal underwear can be a good idea. Most people bring more than they need, causing a stowage problem. A well-organized boat will have designated stowage for each person.

And so it can be seen that an ocean racing yacht is a small world unto itself that must provide the logistics for daily living as part of her function as a racing machine. The organization and planning that go into operating one well can be likened to a military operation. While many a veteran ocean racing sailor cracks cynical jokes about the most complicated way in the world to make yourself uncomfortable and the most involved way possible to proceed at about six miles an hour, there is no denying the hold that distance racing has on its participants. Cold and wet, seasick and tired, sunburned and bleary-eyed, complaining about the measurement rule, their rating, and the weather, they stagger ashore crying, "Never again," repair to the nearest bar, and sign up immediately for the next race, barely able to wait until the starting gun sends them off on the next round of torture.

An ocean racer is a small world unto itself: "Stormvogel" streaking for Bermuda ahead of the fleet

___11

The America's Cup

ALMOST EVERY sport has its one major event—a World Series, Super Bowl, or Kentucky Derby—and the America's Cup is it in sailing. The ornate bottomless mug the schooner *America* brought back from England in 1851 is the Holy Grail of the sailing world. Many other events are important to sailors, but no other has impact outside the sport, and no other has been the object of so many plans, schemes, and daydreams—and such lavish spending.

It is unique for many reasons. It is the oldest international sporting event and has the longest undefeated streak in sports history. It is one of the few major sporting events with all outgo and no income. Millions and millions of dollars have been spent in challenging for it and defending it, yet it has never brought a nickel in gate receipts, or movie or TV rights, to its sponsor. Although it is an international competition in which national pride and prestige are involved, it is actually just a contest between two private clubs. For many years it was competed for by professionals, but it is now an all-amateur event, reversing the trend in many sports. It is virtually unique in sailing competition in being a match race as opposed to a fleet race. Second in most sailing races is a highly respectable finish, but not in the

America's Cup. For years it was the only instance of match racing in sailing, but interest in it, and its influence on sailors, has fostered some other match race events in recent years. It is an event that has usually been harder to qualify for as the defender than to win. The America's Cup series is hardly ever as close as the selection trials preceding it.

America came about as the result of the interest of John Cox Stevens, first commodore of the New York Yacht Club when it was founded in 1844, in developing fast sailboats. His family, for whom Stevens Tech in Hoboken, New Jersey, is named, lived where that institution is now located, at Castle Point, overlooking the Hudson River opposite mid-Manhattan. As we have seen in Chapter 2, from boyhood on, Stevens had experimented with sailboats. His ultimate machine was a ninety-two-foot sloop named *Maria*, based on the Hudson River cargo sloop, which was the fastest thing in the harbor and years ahead of her time in technical developments with her hollow spars; sail tracks and slides; a steering, or balancing, centerboard; and outside ballast in the form of lead strips.

Replica of "America," the schooner that started sailing's most famous competition

Stevens wanted to campaign beyond the confines of New York harbor, but *Maria* was too lightly rigged for offshore work, and he therefore had *America* designed by George Steers for the express purpose of sailing her to England and showing the British how far yachting had come in America. She was based on the swift pilot schooners that operated out of American ports, racing to meet incoming vessels and be first to put a pilot aboard, with a fine, hollowed bow section, her greatest beam just aft of amidships, long, graceful sheer, and a lovely run aft. Her raked masts carried a simple schooner rig. She was 101 feet 9 inches, 90 feet 3 inches on the waterline, and had a beam of 23 feet, 11-foot draft on a long, straight keel, and 5,263 square feet of sail.

She was sailed to Le Havre, France, in twenty days and then outfitted there with racing sails and a gleaming new paint job of black topsides, white spars, and gold cove stripe before sailing across the Channel to Cowes. Unfortunately for Stevens's hopes of arranging match races for good wagers, *America* had an informal brush on arrival with one of the best local boats and walked away from her, and the British sportsmen suddenly turned not so sporting. Finally she was allowed to enter a fifty-mile Royal Yacht Squadron race around the Isle of Wight for the 100 Guinea Cup on August 22. That was an open race, with no handicaps awarded, and fifteen boats met the start in a light westerly off the Squadron clubhouse at Cowes. The start was

"America's" original trailboard and ensign from 1851

The replica "America" making knots at sea

at anchor, and *America* was last in weighing it and squaring away. She quickly caught the fleet, but at the summer residence of Queen Victoria at Osborne House, she was momentarily passed by a British yacht that had picked up a new slant of air. British hearts did not have long to beat faster over this excitement, however. Once the fleet had cleared the Solent and turned westward for a beat along the south shore of the diamond-shaped island, *America* moved rapidly out, footing faster and pointing higher, until she was hull down ahead. Her flat cotton sails were much more efficient than the baggy ones of flax on the British yachts, and her hull form was much better suited to windward work than the bluff-bowed "cod's head and mackerel's tail" shape then in vogue in England.

When she rounded the Needles at the western entrance to the Solent all by herself, she encountered the royal yacht *Britannia* and saluted the Queen by dipping the ensign while the crew doffed caps. That was supposedly the occasion for the Queen's question about who was second and the answer that there was no second, but the story seems apocryphal and has never been substantiated.

America drifted slowly eastward to finish at 2037 in a dying evening breeze, and the British yacht *Aurora,* picking up a fresh sea breeze after dark at the Needles, gained enough to finish eighteen minutes later. If the handicapping system then in use had been applied, *America* would still have saved her time by two minutes.

So newsworthy was the victory that the Queen and her consort made a personal visit to the glossy black vessel sitting jauntily at anchor in Cowes, and English yachtsmen flocked to see the marvel from abroad. Only one boat would try a match race with *America,* though, losing badly. That was her summer.

America's feat has become one of the great legends of sailing, the subject of many articles and books and of a TV special, but it is difficult for modern sailors to put it in perspective. As a result, the unbroken success of the New York Yacht Club in defending the cup has been tainted with accusations of unfair practices and rigged "home town" rules. Even challengers who should have known what they were agreeing to do have tried to build up this impression, completely ignoring the realities of the situation.

America sailed across the ocean and defeated a British fleet under local rules on home waters. At the time, Britain was at the height of its prestige as a world empire and maritime power and also considered itself *the* yachting and social center of the world. It was a tremendous upset, akin to a Little League team winning the World Series, to have a vessel from what had only recently been "the Colonies" invade the world capital of yachting and soundly thrash the cream of the local crop.

It was logical, therefore, for the cup to be donated to the New York Yacht Club on a "Come over and try to take it back" basis, duplicating the conditions under which *America* sailed to victory. When a challenge was received in 1870—the Civil War had held things up for a few years—it was the expected thing to have a single British yacht race a New York Yacht Club fleet on its home course in New York Bay. Despite tides and shoals, that was a much less tricky

The America's Cup in its case at New York YC

course than the one around the Isle of Wight, but the British challenger *Cambria* fared badly, ending seventh on elapsed time and tenth on corrected in a fleet of twenty-three. Since the system was obviously never going to work, the next match saw the American defense fleet reduced to a choice of boats to suit the conditions of the day. That, too, proved disastrous for the British, and they went home mad about the first rhubarb over a protest in the series. It is true that the New York Yacht Club made sure that conditions favored the defender in the matches that followed, since the challenger's specifications were always known before candidates for the defender's berth were built, giving them a natural advantage, and it was also difficult for the challenger to make the ocean voyage across and then fit out for racing, but the trend has always been to ease the requirements for the challenger.

There was an era of particularly hard feeling in the 1890s with Lord Dunraven's two challenges, in which he accused the New York Yacht Club of cheating, engaged in bitter protests, and finally went home in high dudgeon after being stripped of his honorary NYYC membership. It was also the start of the "Herreshoff era," in which Nathanael Herreshoff, the sage of Bristol, Rhode Island, designed every defender from 1893 to 1920. The bad feeling disappeared with the arrival on the scene of Sir Thomas Lipton and his green-hulled *Shamrock*s. Between 1899 and 1930, five of them tried to wrest

"Columbia" leading "Shamrock" in 1899

what he called "the ould mug" from its pedestal in the center of the New York Yacht Club's hushed Trophy Room. None of them came particularly close, but Lipton built an image as one of the most gallant losers in the world of sport, and in the process made his name and his tea a household word.

The *Shamrock*s also spanned the era from the overrigged "skimming dish" machines of the nineties to the stately 130-foot J-boats, the giant sloops of that class under the International Rule in which the competition was held in the thirties. In the depths of the Depression, they were an anachronism of conspicuous consumption and truly marked the end of an era.

"Columbia" became the first repeat cup defender, defeating "Shamrock II" in 1901

Sir Thomas Lipton back for his fifth cup challenge in 1930, greeted in New York by Grover Whalen

The J-boats also saw the closest squeak for the defender in the history of the series. Harold S. Vanderbilt had become the dominant figure on the cup scene with his easy win in *Enterprise* over Lipton's fifth *Shamrock* in 1930, but he almost became the man who let the cup get away in 1934. As skipper of *Rainbow*, designed by Starling Burgess, who had also been responsible for *Enterprise*, Vanderbilt had won a hotly contested selection series against *Yankee* by the margin of one second. The two big sloops had come down on the finish line on a run in what had been announced as the last race in a dying northeaster, with first one and then the other inching ahead momentarily, depending on which one was on the downsurge of a wave. *Rainbow* got the last surge, and the selection, by that one-second edge, about as close as you can come in a sailing race.

J-boats in 1930: a start between "Shamrock V" (left) and "Enterprise"

Her opponent was *Endeavour,* a blue-hulled beauty owned by aircraft tycoon T.O.M. Sopwith (of Sopwith Camel fame), designed by Charles Nicholson. It soon became evident that *Rainbow* had her work cut out for her. Even though *Endeavour* was staffed with an amateur crew, an unheard-of situation in those days of professional "Norwegian steam," she won the first two races on better boat speed. Sopwith had refused to bow to last-minute salary demands of his professionals and had signed on eager amateurs, whose hands were not tough enough, nor muscles hard enough, to do the rugged sail work like Scandinavian professionals. Nevertheless, *Endeavour* had been well enough handled to benefit from her superior speed, and when she took a commanding lead in the third race, a thirty-mile windward-leeward affair, even the most optimistic Americans had all but conceded that the eighty-three-year domination was about to end. Only a miracle could stop *Endeavour* at this stage of the series.

It may not have been a miracle, but a highly improbable set of circumstances did turn things around. Disheartened, and virtually conceding the race and the cup with *Endeavour* leading by 6:39 at the turning mark, Vanderbilt relinquished the wheel and went below. As he always did when that new-fangled sail called a Genoa jib—a big, overlapping monster that had appeared on the sailing scene in Italy in the late twenties and had just been introduced to J-boats—was being used, Vanderbilt turned the wheel over to Sherman Hoyt, probably the world's best racing helmsman in small boats at that time. *Endeavour* also had a genny, but it was an ill-fitting one borrowed from the old American yacht *Vanitie,* and its amateur string-pullers were not at home handling it.

Lying on the deck to leeward so he could watch the luff of the big jib, with the crew's weight carefully distributed on the leeward rail to help keep the sails full in the light air by heeling the hull, Hoyt got *Rainbow* moving well on the edge of a fresher, lifting breeze. *Endeavour* had sagged far to leeward in a hole in the breeze, and Sopwith began to panic at the sight of the white sloop eating up on his quarter. After long hesitation, he made the wrong decision. Instead of waiting for the lift to reach him and fair him for the finish without a tack, he brought the big sloop about onto port tack. In the soft air, with the inexperienced, sore-handed crew on the sheets, the ponderous move killed the boat's way, and *Rainbow* was quite close as the blue boat crossed her bow. Sopwith tacked back on starboard but lost way so badly that *Endeavour* began to sag down on *Rainbow* and had to tack away and then back again. These four agonizingly slow tacks blew her entire lead, as *Rainbow* broke through to leeward and Hoyt kept her in the groove, eating up slowly without tacking until she could fetch the finish, and won going away in 3:26.

The experience so unnerved Sopwith and his crew that the whole effort fell apart. *Endeavour* never sailed up to her potential again, and a series of fouls and protests, which the British lost under recriminations about "homer" decisions, ran out the match. Americans, who had been gloomily conceding the series at the halfway point of the third race, were still pinching themselves in disbelief.

The J-boat era ended in 1937, with Vanderbilt, who had to finance the effort himself in that Depression year, at the helm of one of the most successful racing yachts of all time, *Ranger*. It was the result of a design collaboration between Burgess and young Olin Stephens, and it was also the first cup boat to be tank-tested. The designers used the new and rather primitive facilities at Stevens in Hoboken, virtually on the site of John Cox Stevens's home of the previous century. Primitive or not, they gave *Ranger* a phenomenal jump ahead, and she completely outclassed Sopwith's *Endeavour II*, which had proved faster than the first *Endeavour*, conceded to be the fastest J-boat in existence up to that time.

World War II and the many changes in the sailing, social, and financial worlds that resulted from it and its aftermath seemed to have ended the America's Cup competition forever. Even a Vanderbilt fortune would find it difficult to finance a J in the postwar era, and there seemed no way of reviving the series in smaller boats unless the deed of gift could be changed by legal action. That was accomplished in the fifties under Commodore Harry Sears of the New York Yacht Club, and the 12-Meter era was ushered in, fostering a whole new set of legends and a much wider range of interest around the world. Royal Yacht Squadron put in a challenge for 1958, and the wheels, idle and ungreased since 1937, began to turn on both sides of the ocean.

The 12-Meter was about half as long as a J-boat and much smaller cubically, but it could qualify as the classic racing boat in being at the time, fulfilling the spirit of the competition. It was obvious that a 12 could not come over on its own bottom, and that provision was wiped out.

Unfortunately, the 1958 series was about as one-sided as any in America's Cup history, with the Stephens-designed *Columbia,* sailed by veteran campaigner Briggs Cunningham, crushing the British *Sceptre*, but that did not kill interest in the revival. The American selection series had provided all sorts of excitement, showing what good match racing between evenly matched boats could be like. Two other new boats, *Easterner* and *Weatherly,* were not organized well enough to stand up to *Columbia,* and her toughest fight was against *Vim*, a 1939 12 designed by Stephens for Harold Vanderbilt and used by Stephens as a yardstick in developing *Columbia*. With Bus Mosbacher, whose reputation had been confined largely to Long Island Sound before then, at the wheel, *Vim* gave *Columbia* the most exciting kind of a battle before the improvements Stephens had incorporated in the newer boat finally paid off.

A surprise development in the wake of the humiliation of the British in 1958 was the entry of Australia into the picture in the form of a challenge from Sir Frank Packer, a brash, self-confident publishing tycoon representing Royal Sydney Yacht Squadron. The Aussies were a breath of fresh air and injected all sorts of excitement into what had always been a rather stodgy, tradition-bound set of proceedings. They had to start from absolute scratch, since a 12 had never been designed or built in Australia, and it is a provision that that must be done in the country making the challenge. The New York Yacht Club did allow American sails and other special equipment to be used on *Gretel*. She was designed by Alan Payne, one of the few yacht designers in sparsely populated Australia making a full-time living at the profession. He proved his ability with a dangerously fast boat in his first try. Packer had chartered *Vim* as a trial horse, and the Aussie effort was well mounted and deadly serious beneath the engaging Down Under brashness. Payne worked an impossible schedule not only in designing *Gretel* but in pulling her many details together; the only flaw in the preparations was in Packer's high-handed and impulsive handling of personnel. He refused to pick a skipper until the last minute, stringing two along, so that Jock Sturrock, when he finally got the nod, had not been able to whip the crew into shape himself and had to make do with a last-minute collection that had never sailed together.

The defender was a redesigned and revamped *Weatherly* with the cool, resourceful Mosbacher as skipper, emerging from a fascinating series of races with *Columbia* and the only new boat, Ted Hood's *Nefertiti*.

As the series started before a mammoth spectator fleet that was even bigger than the unbelievable one that had been one of the few excitements of the 1958 scene, it became obvious that in *Gretel*, despite her personnel problems, Payne had come up with a first-rate boat. Lack of coordination in her crew hurt her in the first race and gave Sturrock the chance to get the crew he wanted for the second, which developed into one of the classics of sailing history.

It was sailed in a fresh westerly on a lumpy, whitecapped sea and started with Mosbacher gaining the spot he almost always liked at the start: a safe leeward berth from which he could work the close-winded *Weatherly* up on the other boat's bow, forcing it to tack away. That happened soon after the start, with Mosbacher covering, and one of the most exhausting tacking duels in cup history followed.

Time and again Sturrock slammed *Gretel* over with yoked coffee-grinder winches specially designed by Payne, allowing her crew to trim more quickly in the stiff breeze. With each tack, *Gretel* closed the gap just a mite, and it looked as though she might break through until Mosbacher decided to break it off and give a looser cover, depending on *Weatherly's* ability to live up to her name. His lead was only twelve seconds at the mark, and the boats surged through the next reaching leg as though tied to the same tow rope, while the breeze freshened and seas increased.

The next mark, where the boats jibed for the final run for home of the twenty-four-mile triangle, brought one of the greatest moments of high drama since 1851. *Weatherly* was a bit slow in putting up a spinnaker, and *Gretel,* with her white one bursting out like sculptured marble the instant she squared away on the new jibe, was able to get up on *Weatherly's* port quarter. Just at this moment, she also caught the top of a big Point Judith roller and began to surf for all the world like a planing dinghy. Standing at her mast as he secured the spin- naker halyard, stocky Norm Wright, who had been recruited from Australia's hot eighteen-foot dinghy fleet, felt the big displacement hull quiver and begin to fly just like an "eyedean," as the 18s are called in an Aussie accent. In the 18s, it is traditional for the crews to give a piercing war whoop as a boat hits a plane, and Wright let one out of his barrel chest that almost scared Sturrock out of his helmsman's seat and startled the crew on *Weatherly*, struggling to get their spinnaker full in *Gretel's* wind shadow. As the strange cry crossed the water to them, *Gretel* shot on by to windward and held her lead to the finish, helped by the fact that *Weatherly's* spinnaker guy parted, sending the pole crashing against the headstay and breaking it.

The Aussie victory, tying the series at 1—1, set off one of the monumental celebrations of all time that night in their Newport hangout, a dingy bar called the Cameo, and across the world in the towns and cities of Australia, but the Aussies made another error in strategic organization by sticking to their prearranged plan for a

layday after every race. In that way they missed a carbon-copy day of
fresh westerlies, gave the Americans a chance to regroup their shaken
forces, and ended up losing the third race badly in a light, fitful breeze
that was just to *Weatherly*'s liking. The fourth race was another thril-
ler, but brilliant defensive sailing by Mosbacher held onto a twenty-
six-second lead, smallest margin in cup history. The clincher was
somewhat anticlimactic in an easy *Weatherly* win, but the whole
series had generated more excitement than anyone could have
imagined, setting the stage for some more Aussie fireworks in the future.

The British, squeezed out by Packer's surprise challenge, were
given a chance in 1964, selecting their challenger from two identically
hulled designs—*Kurrewa* and *Sovereign,* from *Sceptre*'s designer
David Boyd—in the first election series for a challenger ever held in
American waters. Unfortunately, that extra competition did them no
good whatsoever, as the latest Stephens creation, *Constellation*, won
by embarrassingly large margins. The only moment of drama came at
the start of the first race, when Bob Bavier maneuvered *Constellation*
into a split-second start that left *Sovereign* wallowing in her wake.
The excitement of the summer came in the selection duel between
Constellation and *American Eagle. Eagle* was from the design board
of Bill Luders, who had had a large hand in the revamping of Phil
Rhodes's original design for *Weatherly* in 1962, and she won twelve
straight races at the start of the trials. *Connie* had had shakedown
troubles, but Bavier took her helm in midsummer and got her moving
in one of the most exciting come-from-behind stories in sailing.

Mosbacher came back to action in 1967, when the Aussies once
again challenged. This time, he was linked with Olin Stephens in a
new design for the first time, and the result, *Intrepid*, was as
unbeatable as *Ranger* had been twenty years previously. She walked
away with the selection trials and handled Jock Sturrock in the
Warwick Hood-designed *Dame Pattie* just as easily. *Intrepid* had
such innovations for 12s as a short keel, separate rudder, and

below-deck winches, and everyone called her the superboat of all 12s.

When *Intrepid* defeated *Gretel II* in 1970, she became the first defender to repeat since *Columbia* in 1899-1901, but *Intrepid* didn't do it in superboat fashion, and the match produced more oddities and controversy than any since at least Lord Dunraven's time. *Intrepid* was taken over by a new syndicate, and her afterbody was reworked by young designer Britton Chance. With Bill Ficker at the helm, she won the selection over *Valiant,* the first new boat by Olin Stephens to fail as a defense candidate since the 12-Meter revival, and Charlie Morgan's outclassed *Heritage* from Florida.

There was a strong body of opinion that *Intrepid* was slower with her new underbody than she had been in 1970, and she was certainly a more sluggish boat, with poorer acceleration and maneuvering characteristics. She was well handled and well organized, however, and the obvious choice as defender. Alan Payne had produced a fast, lively boat for Sir Frank Packer in *Gretel II,* and it was probably the first time in one hundred years of challenges that the series was settled on the water rather than ahead of time on the design board and in the sail lofts and machine shops of America. The technology gap had been closed, and it developed into match racing at its very best.

Gretel had earned the challenger's berth after the first sail-off for that position in cup history. France had also entered a challenge, from ballpoint pen tycoon Baron Marcel Bich with the Andre Mauric-designed *France,* which had been tested against a Chance-designed trial horse, *Chancegger,* which was not eligible as a challenger since Chance was not a Frenchman. *France* had a strong resemblance to the trial horse but was no match for the Aussies. If Packer's personnel moves had been erratic in 1962, Bich's were positively zany, and *France* never managed to show anything. The climax of its 4—0 loss to *Gretel* came in a bizarre, fog-enshrouded race in which Bich, in formal wear, yachting cap, and white gloves, took over the wheel himself and proceeded to get lost in the fog. His recriminations were long and angry as he railed against the International Race Committee

"Intrepid," winner in 1967 and 1970, and almost defender again in 1974

for conducting the race in the fog, but they remained comic opera to everyone else. The series was an innovation permitted by New York Yacht Club in an attempt to give the challenger more combat experience before meeting the defender.

There were all sorts of weird occurrences in the *Intrepid-Gretel II* match, including a man overboard (quickly recovered) from *Gretel* in the stormy first race; a protest by both boats before the start of it, the first in cup action since 1934; the first race abandonment, called because of fog in the second race after *Gretel* had led at the first mark of the first leg but was passed under spinnaker; the first Sunday race in cup history; the removal of Ficker's invaluable tactician, Steve Van Dyck, by helicopter from *Intrepid* on the way out to the Sunday start for treatment of a violent reaction to a bee sting; a supposed floating mine, in among the mammoth spectator fleet, that turned out to be a fishnet float; an amazing come-from-behind win by *Gretel* when *Intrepid* seemed to have the series sewed up in the fourth race; the longest duration *ever* for a cup series, fourteen days; and The Foul. Amid all the rest of the excitement, this incident in the second race caused the biggest uproar in 119 years of cup history.

Never has there been so much discussion of sailing in non-nautical circles and from so many ill-informed and downright ignorant self-appointed experts. It all started when Martin Visser, who had been given the responsibility of making *Gretel's* starts before her skipper, Jim Hardy, took over the wheel for the rest of the race, tried to luff *Intrepid* up at the start. *Gretel* was to leeward of *Intrepid* as Ficker brought the defender in toward the line in what would be a barging action if *Gretel* could close the gap before the gun went off. As they did (without success) in the first race, evidently as a calculated tactic, the Aussies were trying to force a fouling situation, but *Gretel* was not moving fast enough to cut *Intrepid* off at the committee boat. As the gun went off, there was room for Ficker to squeeze through, since *Gretel* was no longer permitted, under Rule 42.1 (e), to luff above close-hauled. Evidently under the impression that the buoy-room rule for rounding marks of the course after the start applied in this case, Visser continued to luff above close-hauled after the gun until *Gretel's* bow hit *Intrepid* just abaft the chainplates (and left her bowpieces on the American deck). *Gretel's* protest flag went up immediately and was answered by one on *Intrepid*, which had swept on through to a good lead as *Gretel*, with less way on, wallowed in her wake.

Ironically, if Visser had observed the rule and squared away on a close-hauled heading with the gun, instead of continuing to luff, he could have turned the wheel over to Hardy with *Gretel* in a safe leeward position and in command. Eventually, in the direct run of the 24.3-mile Olympic-type course of triangle, windward-leeward-windward, better downwind tacking angles permitted *Gretel* to pass the Van Dyck-less *Intrepid*, and the spectator fleet, not knowing about the protests, went wild with excitement over the supposed 1—1 tie in the series.

When the committee, headed by B. Devereux Barker, Jr., announced, after the most careful hearings and overnight deliberations, that *Gretel* had been disqualified under 42.1 (e), the repercussions were instantaneous and loud. With no new evidence and no change in facts, Packer tried to get rehearings twice and fought the subject in the press for days, making insinuations about NYYC's "own rules" (the rules were the International Yacht Racing Union ones that are used for all formal sailing events everywhere). Politicians and ambassadors took up the cry and made critical statements, and one Australian politician suggested withdrawing Ausie troops from Vietnam, but none of them knew anything about the sailing rules, which had been correctly interpreted.

Ficker won the third race by controlling the start and protecting his lead by masterful downwind tacking on the last run. He seemed to have a 4—0 series wrapped up when he rounded the last mark of the fourth race with a 1:02 lead. The leg looked as though it could almost be a fetch, so *Intrepid* tacked immediately instead of standing on to windward at all, but she was gradually headed, while *Gretel,* well back on her starboard quarter, picked up a new lift and began eating up to windward in somewhat the same situation as the *Endeavour-Rainbow* finish that turned the 1934 series around. *Intrepid* tacked over too late in an attempt to cover and lost the lead and the race by the same time margin she had held at the previous mark, and the closest distance—about fifty yards of agonized wallowing—since boat-for-boat racing was first used in cup races.

That meant a fifth race after three days' delay, and it was one of the real classics of match race infighting, as Hardy (not Visser) got the start and held a slight lead up the first leg in a light, shifty northerly. *Intrepid* broke through the cover in a tacking duel when Hardy chose to tack under her lee bow, rather than cross while on port tack, and got caught there by a shift that lifted *Intrepid* high enough for her to

"Courageous" rides over a stalling "Southern Cross" (KA 4) in a 1974 start

hold control. From then on, Ficker fought a masterful defensive battle against the more quickly accelerating *Gretel* and came out of an agonizingly long, slow downwind tacking duel on the last run with a twenty-second margin that she held to the finish, helped by a slight lift right after rounding the mark onto starboard tack, while *Gretel* was standing into the slant on port tack.

It had been the most exciting, most discussed series of all, and it was a let-down in 1974 to go back to the old pattern of a tense, dramatic selection series followed by a decisive victory for the defender—especially so because another brash Aussie challenger, real estate developer Alan Bond, put on an intense public relations campaign stressing complete confidence in an Australian victory. The deflation of this balloon was one of the worst anticlimaxes in the whole America's Cup story.

Courageous, in which Olin Stephens had gone back to the design thread that had been developed through *Vim-Columbia-Constellation-Intrepid,* and ignoring the flyer he had taken with the full-bodied *Valiant,* was an easy victor over Bond's *Southern Cross. Cross* was the first 12 from Aussie designer Bob Miller and had Jim Hardy as skipper again, while Ted Hood ended up as the skipper of *Courageous* after a summer of trials that were as dramatic as the *Yankee-Rainbow, Vim-Columbia,* and *American Eagle-Constellation* battles, or more so. *Intrepid* was back again, sailed by a West Coast crew, with Jerry Driscoll as skipper and a Seattle Sailing Foundation, supported in part by public subscription, as her sponsor.

Since aluminum had been approved for 12-Meter construction, and the consensus was that that would outmode all wooden boats because of more efficient weight distribution, *Intrepid* was the preseason underdog to *Courageous* and the Chance-designed *Mariner,* with ocean racing star Ted Turner as skipper. *Mariner* proved to be one of the all-time busts in cup history, however, as her radical stern section did not work at all and had to be replaced, still without success, and *Intrepid* put up such a good fight against *Courageous* that the series was continued to the last possible day before the selection had to be made. Bob Bavier had brought *Courageous* this far through many ups and downs and increasingly tense pressures from her syndicate, only to be relieved for the last race by sailmaker-designer-ocean racing skipper Ted Hood, who had been aboard as tactician. Aided by a gear failure on *Intrepid* in the strong breeze of the last race, Hood sailed *Courageous* to victory and the selection. With West Coast hotshot Dennis Conner taking over as starting helmsman, she completely demolished *Southern Cross* in four easy races.

The resurgence of overwhelming American superiority might have been cause for discouragement among challenging nations, but such is the lure of the America's Cup and its legends that four countries immediately jumped into the lists for 1977 at the conclusion of the *Southern Cross* debacle. Australia, England, and France, which had sent *France* over for a token appearance against *Southern Cross* in the challenge selection series, all signed up, and a newcomer to the cup history, Sweden, also entered a challenge, promising yet another fascinating chapter in the 125-year-old saga of the "ould mug."

PART III

CRUISING AND DAY SAILING

___12

Day Sailing

RACING, with its competitive tensions, rules, sophisticated equipment, and total involvement of participants, is a world unto itself, and an important part of sailing. Few are the sailors, or any human beings for that matter, who don't react to a competitive urge at some time in their lives. For every racing sailor, however, there are many more who look on sailing as a release from the tensions of competition, its demands, and its disciplines. For them, sailing means freedom from all this, a chance to get away from the pressures of daily living; and there is, in truth, no better way to do it.

There is always a challenge in dealing with nature, and there must be a sense of responsibility to the safety of those involved and to the condition of the equipment. There is not quite the free and easy passivity of lying in front of TV and munching chocolates in going cruising or day sailing, but it is a world apart that has tangible, and very welcome, rewards, without excess pressure or demands.

Day sailing, the simplest form of getting afloat without the involvement of competition, needs no great manual of do's and don't's. It is not a complicated activity, and once the basics of how to handle a boat under sail, as outlined in Chapter 4, are mastered, the ingredients are all there for many pleasant hours afloat. However, there are some points to make on the type of boat and equipment to use and the best way to get the most out of the activity.

The most important point is: keep it simple. To get the most rewarding fun out of day sailing, the boat should be easy to handle, safe, sturdy, and reliable, and her equipment should be simple and functional.

The Boat

A day sailer can be anything from the smallest boardboat up to a 12-Meter—some people have bought 12-Meters that are outmoded for competition and used them as day sailers. That they must be, as they do not have accommodations unless expensive alterations are made, and even an outmoded 12 can provide exciting, exhilarating sailing, just the pure joy of going fast under sail.

This would be the extreme, however, and the smaller end of the scale is much more heavily populated. Just messing around in a boardboat has probably put more people afloat under sail than any other form of sailing. No other type of sailboat can provide a stronger feeling of being at one with wind and water than a boardboat. You are practically an integral part of the slender craft, and every one of its reactions can be felt immediately. You have to move your weight instantly in reaction to puffs, you are as wet as the hull itself, and you often capsize with no real damage done to anything but dignity. This is sailing at its most elemental, a close physical involvement. There is no better way to get the feel of a sailboat than to hack around in a boardboat. Mistakes cause little trouble, since they are easily rectified, and the basic maneuvers like tacking and jibing can be repeated as often as desired until they become natural and almost automatic. And coaxing a boardboat onto a screaming plane is one of the real thrills of sailing.

A word of caution: novices should not take a boardboat onto open waters in an offshore wind if they have not acquired confidence enough to beat back to shore against the breeze. Especially if the wind is puffy and uneven, which it is likely to be when blowing from land toward open water, boardboats can be difficult to bring about and tend to get into irons quite easily.

That is a good point to remember in any kind of day sailing. Always think about the eventual return to home when you take off. The euphoria of a pleasant run or reach on the early part of a sail may change to chagrin and frustration if the return trip becomes a slow beat or a long push against a foul tide.

Boardboats and vessels as sophisticated as a 12-Meter can be day sailers (the famous seventy-three-foot ocean racer *Ticonderoga* was originally built as a "comfortable family day sailer" with a minimum of accommodations). However, a general category of boat comes to mind when the type is mentioned: a sloop or catboat in the fourteen-to-twenty-foot range with a comfortable, roomy cockpit. She would sail well without the need for top performance, be relatively dry and stable, handle without a great amount of sail-trimming and sheet-tending, have a modicum of storage space, perhaps have provision for outboard auxiliary power, be easy to maintain, and have a simple rig.

In selecting a day sailer, look for sturdy, simple fittings. She need not have superlight (and superexpensive) turnbuckles, blocks, and cleats. Sheets should be led for ease of handling and for least interference with passengers and skipper. In a racing boat, the best lead for the mainsheet might be right to the floorboards in the center of the cockpit, but a day sailer can have the whole mainsheet assembly at the after end of the cockpit so that it doesn't cut across anyone on the seats. The seats should be roomy and comfortable, with a good backrest, wide seating area, and plenty of leg room. Most day sailers should probably be centerboarders, depending on the local area; it is a convenience to be able to go into shallow water, pull up on a beach, and, in many cases, have a trailable boat. If the area is

Sporty boardboats like the Sunfish are the simplest kind of day sailer

Day sailing can be relaxed or a real workout like this group having fun in an E Sloop Inland Lake scow

Catboats make roomy, comfortable day sailers

This nineteen-foot sloop, an O'Day Mariner, is a typical day sailer

one of deep waters and no need for shallow operations, lack of a centerboard does allow more room in the cockpit. Suit the boat to your area.

A pleasant feature for a day sailer is some form of cuddy cabin or enclosed area under the foredeck. Especially if children are to be a part of the crew fairly often, it is a great plus to have a place where they can curl up for a nap, "play house," or stay out of a sudden rain squall or cold wind. It can also be a good stowage area for such items as foul-weather gear, life jackets, picnic equipment, and radio.

For simple day sailing, avoid boats with running backstays, oversize jibs requiring winches for trimming, and complicated gear for adjusting luff tension on jib and mainsail. A club-footed, self-trimming jib is a great convenience in day sailing, since the jib sheets need not be trimmed at all while tacking.

Auxiliary Motor

Depending on the area and the intended scope of operations, auxiliary power is a great plus for a day sailer. Small, light outboard motors, some especially designed for sailboat use, are on the market. It is better to have an outboard than an inboard engine as a day sailer auxiliary, mainly to save cockpit space, not to mention initial expense. Most day sailers can get along perfectly well with a motor in the 3.5-to-7.5-horsepower range, light and easily handled. Transom brackets are the best method of mounting the motor. Brackets are usually adjustable, so that the motor can be raised and tipped up when not in use. The portable tanks of outboards make refueling easy, and the motor's portability means that it can be taken ashore for stowage and service with a minimum of fuss. Don't be misled into buying a bigger than necessary motor. Except for the biggest, heaviest boats in the day sailer class, the 8-horsepower range, with a weight under sixty pounds, is the absolute top needed, and the smaller, lighter motors are usually more satisfactory. The ability to come home on schedule despite lack of wind or foul tide and to get out of confined slips, piers with foul currents, or areas too shallow for sailing makes an auxiliary motor almost indispensable.

Trailing

Trailing behind the family car adds an invaluable extra dimension to day sailing, and it might also solve the problem of where to keep a boat. Parking a boat in one's driveway is a happy answer to the berthing problem. In addition to saving expense in mooring fees, maintenance is simplified, and security worries are minimized. There is also a great advantage in the expanded horizons opened up by a boat's trailability. Each junket can be to a new body of water, and the vagaries of weather can be thwarted by heading for an area with the best reports.

Most day sailers—except deep keel boats, which are in the minority, as mentioned above—are well suited to trailing. A rig that can be raised and lowered with a minimum of difficulty (with a deck tabernacle for the mast) and an underwater shape that adapts easily to a trailer are important factors in trailability. The car should be fitted out for trailing with a permanent, strong hitch (not just a bumper hitch) and adapters for brake and stop lights. Most dealers who sell trailers can install these adaptations or recommend a shop that does. Sometimes, in equipping for trailing heavy boats, it is necessary to provide connections for brakes on the trailer from the tow car, but that is not always a necessity with lighter day sailers.

Equipment

Day sailers should, of course, have the required safety equipment for the class of boat and other absolutely necessary items like anchor and line, pump or bailer, local charts, compass, binoculars, radio, tool kit, flashlights, rigging spares, and first-aid kit. Except in the most limited operations, like boardboat sailing in a bathing suit, the extra items are of paramount importance. A radio can keep the kids happy with their favorite disc jockey (if the parents can stand it), but it is also a must for weather reports. If you are in an area that provides government weather broadcasts on VHF, you can at least carry one of the simple, inexpensive sets that are solely tuned to this type of broadcast.

Depending on the size of boat, it can be very pleasant if the equipment list also includes an ice chest or Scotch cooler; a minimal water supply, even if it is only a plastic bottle or two; and, if your operations are likely to be day-long, some form of toilet, whether it be cedar bucket, plastic pail, or portable chemical head.

Operational Hints

Day sailing is a scaled-down form of cruising, and some of the same considerations apply. The most important one is: don't try to do too much. A junket that starts out pleasantly and ends up with a long push home through cold twilight breezes or a buggy calm can leave a negative impression that wipes out all the earlier pleasures of the day.

Plan ahead. Check your equipment before you start. Has anything been used that needs replacing? Is everything operable? Enough fuel? Ice? Water? Do you have enough life jackets for the number of people aboard? Check the weather. It may look great at 0900, but what will the afternoon bring? What is the tide doing? When will the current change? (Those may be separate items in tidal waters.)

While underway, pick the points of sailing that will be the most pleasant for the type of crew you have with you. Don't slug out a hard chance to windward with passengers unused to sailing and unlikely to enjoy spray down their necks. Figure out the whole day so the end of it doesn't leave you in a difficult spot for getting home comfortably. Especially if children are involved, pick a target or a theme for the day: some special place to sightsee or spot to land for a picnic, some cove to explore or race to watch. Don't make children sit still so long that it becomes an ordeal for them. Break up the day by anchoring for a marshmallow roast or a visit to an interesting spot. Let them steer and tend sails when they want to without making great demands of them. Whatever your crew, relax and enjoy it. That's what day sailing's all about.

_13

Cruising Boats

CRUISING under sail has become one of the most popular aspects of the world of sailing. More cabin auxiliaries are built for this purpose than for any other, and a whole special breed of boat has developed. Racing came before cruising in the early days of pleasure sailing. Cruising was a hit-or-miss, individualistic affair for adventurous souls who weren't afraid to set out on their own, as few facilities catered to them, there were no special guidebooks other than government publications intended for commercial shipping, and the boat was usually an adaptation of a commercial type or some tired fugitive from the racing front.

The author's former boat "Mar Claro" was an early example of a trailable and had convertible hood to give head-room

This state of affairs lasted until well after World War I. Long voyagers at the turn of the century, like Joshua Slocum, Captain Voss, and their imitators, proved that small sailboats could make long passages by completing global circumnavigations and transoceanic passages, but their voyages were looked upon as stunts and were commercially inspired. Some large yachts with big professional crews also engaged in long cruises, but these were millionaire junkets on a grand scale with little relation to the type of cruising popular today.

Cruising is a way of getting from one place to another, but though it is a descendant of passages from the days when sail was the only means of crossing oceans, it is certainly not efficient transportation. You can get there faster by almost any other means. Cruising is the ultimate escape afloat, a state of mind, a way of life, and a peculiar form of challenge. Instead of the pressures of competition, this is a challenge from nature to harness its forces and get the better of them in one of man's most elemental contests. Harbors, no matter how undistinguished, take on special significance, an aura of glamour that is almost mystical, when they are achieved after a passage under sail. It can be for an afternoon or a month, but the same reward is there. The vessel is a tiny world unto itself, transporting her occupants completely out of the rest of the world beyond the horizon or the point of land that lies on it. The horizon is the lure, no matter how limited or how wide, whether it leads to a cove just around the next point or the islands of the South Pacific.

As in every other form of sailing, cruising can be what you choose to make it: a jaunt to that next cove or a rounding of Cape Horn, a winter in the Caribbean, a week's cruise to Catalina, a weekend on Cuttyhunk, or gunkholing the North Channel. It attracts adventurers who don't care if they see land for weeks at a time, and it delights luxury-lovers who are happy as long as the boat is plugged in to a marina, with a gourmet restaurant at the head of the slip.

In the early days of cruising, the boats were makeshifts. Few were designed solely for cruising. In the decade after World War I,

The author's cruising boat—a Morgan Out Island 36 with tri-cabin, center cockpit layout, roller furling jib, and bow-chock anchor

however, when Boston-based John Alden began adapting designs for yachts from New England fishing schooner types, some of them were raced and, as we have seen, did especially well in the early Bermuda Race. They also, however, made roomy, sturdy cruising boats, well-suited to New England conditions, whose popularity was widespread and very influential. Cruising gained many devotees in that era.

For the next fifty years or so, cruising and racing were compatible functions for one boat. Carleton Mitchell could campaign *Finisterre* as the top ocean racing yacht of the fifties, winning the Bermuda Race three times, and still use her as an extremely comfortable and well-thought-out cruising boat. He sailed her across the Atlantic on a cruise, and he spent months aboard her in the Bahamas cruising in comfort, and in fact outright luxury, with such amenities as mechanical refrigeration, large water and fuel tanks, and a beautifully paneled and appointed interior. Almost every major auxiliary was designed with racing and cruising in mind, unless it was an out-and-out motor sailer, with no pretensions to racing capability.

That dual-purpose approach to auxiliaries lasted through the sixties, when profound changes in the approach to both ocean racing and cruising made it almost impossible to design a boat that would be good at both. The introduction of the IOR formula for measuring ocean racers led to the development of machines that were completely unsuitable for cruising, and there was also an increasingly sophisticated awareness of the characteristics necessary for ocean racing success. Weight became the villain and had to be reduced in everything but ballast. Cabin paneling, enclosed heads, extra refrigeration, tanks, bunkboards, and such items as water-pressure systems—all were deemed excess weight in an ocean racer. In addition, weight in the ends of a boat—at the bow and stern—was also taboo, making cruising amenities like an anchor stowed in the bow and a roomy lazarette for extra stowage in the stern impossible to combine with racing efficiency. A good racing boat should concentrate all weight possible amidships, while a good cruising boat should make best possible use for comfort of all space.

Almost simultaneously with this new thinking in ocean racers came a major development in the cruising field. The economic boom of the sixties, combined with a great increase in sailboat ownership and the opening of the jet age in air travel, produced a new form of cruising: bareboat chartering in southern waters. Experienced owners who had the knowledge and money to spend a sailing vacation in the Bahamas or Caribbean, but not the time to get their own boats there, could charter a boat especially set up for bareboating for a week or two. In bareboating, the charter party runs the boat without benefit of paid crew. That type of operation increased rapidly, with commercial fleets established in the Bahamas, Virgins, and Lesser Antilles, in the late sixties and early seventies, and it also brought about development of boats designed and intended totally for cruising. Racing was forgotten, and the new breed of boat was strictly a machine for cruising comfort, in its own way just as specialized a machine as the new ocean racers.

Many an ocean racer-cruiser from pre-IOR days lasted into this era as a well-suited cruising boat, and of course there were boats designed solely for cruising all through the fifty years in which racing and cruising were normally combined, but a whole new concept of what a cruising sailboat should and could be also developed. Sometimes it is called a *full-cruising boat* or a *full-powered* auxiliary. The latter is meant as a differentiation from a motor sailer in that the design was intended to perform well on all points of sailing while still being capable of good speed under power. Motor sailers, by very broad and unspecific definition, are closer to powerboats, with sails that can be a help in downwind work, but not capable of all-around sailing performance. Owners of full-cruising boats are usually highly insulted if their boat is dubbed a motor sailer.

The complete split between cruising and racing is most pronounced from thirty feet up. In boats under thirty feet, it is easier and more successful to combine racing ability with cruising comfort. There isn't room for the heavy amenities possible in larger boats: water-pressure systems, deep freezes, extra-large tanks, showers, air conditioning, and other such delights. All-out racing machines are produced in this range, such as the smaller Ton classes, but a boat that a young family can use for a vacation cruise can also double in organized racing competition and still stand a chance.

The capacity of a cruising boat is always a key question. Originally, most cruising boats were custom designed and built, and each owner could work out his own requirements. After the fiberglass revolution of the fifties and sixties, the pendulum swung over to mass production of stock boats, and each manufacturer therefore tried to give his boat as high a capacity as sounded reasonable. What is reasonable is another question.

It is possible to crowd a great many bunks into a small space. The Dougal Robertson family, in its remarkable survival saga after its yacht was sunk by a whale in mid-Pacific, managed to exist for thirty-seven days with six people (two of them were children) in an eight-foot raft, but no manufacturer has gone quite so far in making claims for the capacity of his product as a sleeper. Unfortunately, some do put more places for people to sleep in a boat than the boat can sensibly handle in any other way. There must be a viable relationship between bunk capacity and the room needed for dressing, brushing one's teeth, cooking, stowing clothes and gear, and moving around, without looking like the Marx Brothers in the celebrated stateroom scene in *A Night at the Opera*.

There is no hard-and-fast rule on capacity in relation to overall length, but some sensible guidelines can be used, and it would take considerable ingenuity to exceed them. That applies to maximum permanent cabin accommodations. There can always be one night or a weekend when someone curls up in a sleeping bag in the cockpit, or children double up in one adult-sized bunk.

Size	Permanent Bunks
Up to 22 feet	2
22-28 feet	4
28-30 feet	5
30-38 feet	6
38 and up	8 or more

A thirty-footer like this Hinckley Sou'Wester Jr. is comfortable for four, can handle five

Five in a boat under thirty feet, and eight anywhere under forty feet, is possibly stretching it a bit, but it has been done with some degree of success. At all times, it is better to underload than overload, and the makeup of the crew has much to do with how the sleeping capacity works out. Different considerations apply for groups with children from those with all middle-aged, comfort-loving, and privacy-loving adults. In a boat of any size, being limited to one head is a problem for any capacity over four people.

A separate category of cruising boat has become very popular in recent years: the trailable. Boats up to about twenty-six feet have been developed that are intended for dry-land storage and trailing behind the average family car. With the shortage of facilities for in-water mooring in many areas, notably southern California, and the spread of boating interest to inland areas located at some distance from good cruising areas, the only way a good many sailors can manage to go cruising is in a trailable.

Horizons are greatly expanded by the trailable. Someone with limited vacation time, who would normally be unable to move his boat by water more than a couple of hundred miles from home base, can make the whole continent his oyster by driving the boat to a distant cruising ground in a day or two. Facilities exist at many yards and marinas for launching trailable boats, and they can even be used as house trailers for overnighting aboard while on the road.

A trailable boat should not have a deep keel, and it should be relatively light in weight, with an underbody that conforms easily to sitting and riding on a trailer. Outboard power cuts down on weight and on extrusions such as propeller and skeg that make trailing more difficult. Most trailables are what is known as *swing keel* boats. A swing keel is a retractable plate, like a centerboard, but weighted to provide the ballast a cruising boat should have, and raised and lowered by a winch with a good power ratio. Sloop rigs that can easily be lowered and raised from a cabin-top tabernacle and stowed on deck are another must. Florida for one vacation, Maine the next, and the Great Lakes another time are not impossibilities with trailables.

The characteristics of other types of cruising boats should be considered in several categories: hull form, rig, auxiliary power, and accommodations.

Hull Forms

The split between ocean racers and full-cruising boats starts with the type of hull favored for each. Since ocean racers are concerned with the last split-second of speed potential, wetted surface and the friction it creates become a problem. One way to reduce wetted surface is to separate rudder and keel and to use short fin keels rather than ones that run the length of the underbody. Short keels also make a boat livelier in response to the helm.

They do not, however, make her comfortable in a seaway. For maximum seakindliness and steering control, a long, relatively shallow keel with the rudder attached to it well aft on the underbody is much the best, especially desirable in a cruising boat. In racing, there is always someone on the helm concentrating on the most minute nuances of helmsmanship and boat speed, and the helmsman is alternated often to avoid fatigue and lack of attention. Cruising boats are not necessarily stocked with hot-racing helmsmen, and, while no one advocates a goof-off, it does make for a much pleasanter cruising passage if the helmsman can light a cigarette, use the binoculars, or take a peek at the chart without having the boat spin out of control.

A full, strong hull with easy lines and relatively well-rounded bilges also gives a cruising boat better stability and a generally more comfortable ride when a sea is running, easy and fluid as opposed to quick and jerky.

Wide beam, good freeboard and headroom, and moderate draft are other characteristics important in a cruising boat if well handled by

Multihulls are capable of great speed on certain points of sailing. This trimaran is making sixteen knots

the designer. Beam and freeboard provide more living space and better stowage, as far as living comfort is concerned. If incorporated in a proper design, they can also contribute to stability and dryness, both very important in a cruising boat. While deep draft may be a benefit in relation to seakeeping ability, especially if a boat is intended for offshore purposes, it is a limiting factor in a boat intended for coastwise cruising. Many cruising grounds have shallow waters as their highlights, and deep draft boats cannot enjoy them. This is particularly true of southern New England, Chesapeake Bay, the Bahamas, the Gulf of Mexico, and some areas of the Great Lakes, as well as parts of the intracoastal waterway system. Over five feet is quite limiting and, for a combination of seakeeping ability and manageable draft for shallow areas, the three-and-a-half-to-four-and-a-half-foot range is about right. Addition of a centerboard can sometimes add to the sailing capability of a boat in the shallower range, though it can also be a nuisance in maintenance and operational problems.

With fiberglass the almost universal construction material, round-bottomed designs are predominant. Hard chines made for easier and cheaper construction in wood, but there is no need for this in fiberglass, aluminum, or ferro-cement, the three most frequently encountered construction materials. Virtually all stock boats have been built of fiberglass since the late sixties, although aluminum is sometimes specified for premium custom boats. Ferro-cement has had a vogue because of its supposed cheapness and adaptibility to home construction. It does have these advantages if handled correctly, but inexperienced amateurs can botch a ferro-cement job with incorrect procedures, especially in the curing of the cement, and serious corrosion problems can result.

So far we have been talking about monohulls, and by far the greatest number of boats are single-hulled, but catamarans and trimarans are used as cruising boats too. Multihulls are particularly attractive to home builders, as cost can be held down for a given length since inexpensive materials like plywood can be used, and the boats are lighter for their length than monohulls. Since multihulls have less wetted surface and offer less resistance with their easily driven hulls, they can achieve higher speeds than monohulls under certain conditions. They are potentially faster off the wind, but not as able to windward.

Two major problems with multihulls have led to a high percentage of accidents in offshore passaging. Catamarans and trimarans have made circumnavigations and other long open-water voyages under difficult conditions, including a west-east rounding of Cape Horn by Colin and Rosie Swale of England, with their two babies along. Theirs was a thirty-foot catamaran. However, the tremendous stresses between the separate hulls of multihulls can lead to failure of the cross-braces, and they have been known to break up when driven too hard. Also, they easily capsize and then can't be righted. A ballasted monohull can suffer a knockdown, but provided she still has water-tight integrity, she will right herself safely. Once a multihull loses her great initial stability, which is a plus factor in comfort, and flips, it is over for good. For that reason, it is not safe to put multihulls on self-steering without someone on watch to tend sheet at all times.

Another disadvantage of multihulls is that they take up so much space with their wide beam that it is difficult to find berths for them, or anchoring space, in crowded harbors. In most marinas, slips are for monohulls and can't accommodate the wider craft.

Multihull devotees are fanatics, and there are sailors who say they would never go back to a monohull after experiencing the pleasures of multihull sailing, but they are a small minority in the whole field of cruising sailors.

Rigs

Cruising boats can be found in a variety of rigs, but sloops and cutters predominate, with ketches next and then small numbers of yawls, catboats, schooners, and such oddball affairs as Chinese lug rigs and cat ketches.

Catboats are suitable in the smaller range of cruising boats (which is the larger range of catboat). The single sail is an advantage in simplicity of handling, but a disadvantage in a blow in that it must be reefed to reduce sail area, while a boat with multiple sails can merely take one or more off. For their overall length, catboats have excellent room and provide great comfort for their size. An eighteen-foot catboat can be the equivalent of a twenty-two-foot sloop or more in usable space, though it is difficult to obtain more than sitting headroom. Stability and shallow draft are other catboat pluses. Their beam makes them comfortable in good breezes, and low draft permits gunkholing few other cruising boats can do. Above twenty-two feet, the single sail of a catboat is too big to handle safely. The cat ketch is a fairly rare rig in which the mainmast is all the way forward, with no room for jibs. Its major advantage is simplicity in a divided rig.

Sloops and cutters are popular as cruising rigs because they combine relative simplicity with an efficient sail plan and one that can be reduced in a blow with ease. Cost is also less than for boats with more than one mast, since each mast, and its rigging and extra sails, adds to total expense. As boat size increases, the single-stick rig loses its advantage, since the sails then become too big to be manageable. There is no demarcation line at which experts concur that it is better to have a divided rig. Under thirty feet, a divided rig can look salty and cute, but it isn't very efficient. Through the thirties, there can be arguments on the merits of both, though a single-stick still makes more sense. Over forty feet, a divided rig should have definite advantages, and over fifty feet a single-stick is a pretty big rig for cruising. All divided rigs add weight and windage as well as expense.

A piece of equipment that came into popular use with the development of full cruising boats in the late sixties is the roller-furling jib, one which can be rolled up on its own luff wire like a vertical window-shade when not in use and broken out again in the wink of an eye. That makes shortening sail so easy and quick that sloops up to forty feet can be safely handled by a man and wife. Roller-furling mains have been coming gradually into use as well, and they add even more to the ease and safety with which a sloop or cutter can be handled, though their efficiency leaves something to be desired. A cutter, as opposed to a sloop, is called that because it generally has a larger foretriangle, with the mast stepped farther aft, and multiple jibs can be used, again providing a means of changing sail area by steps when wind strength varies.

Another rig variation that has been a boon to cruising boats, especially on long passages in following winds, is the practice of winging out two jibs on special poles rather than tending a spinnaker, and specially designed equipment can be bought for this purpose.

Ketches have always been favored by cruising yachtsmen because of the flexibility of the rig. Sail area can be added or reduced in small, multiple doses, with each step easy to handle. A favorite combination is *jib and jigger*. When the breeze gets too strong to carry full sail, lowering the main and proceeding under the jib and mizzen—also called *jigger*—makes the boat safely manageable. In light air, it is possible to add staysails forward of the mizzen and increase area for downwind work. In a ketch, the mizzen is not too much smaller than the mainsail, since the mizzen mast is forward of the rudder post, and flexibility of rig is paid for by reduction in windward ability. The ketch rig is not *especially* close-winded in a cruising boat, although some maxi ocean racers have been rigged as ketches simply because they have plenty of room for a big mizzen for carrying added sail area downwind. With big mainsails and foretriangles, they are really racing sloops with a separate rig added aft for extra sail area, and they are a far cry from the average cruising ketch. If you want a cruising boat with the ultimate in a manageable rig, a ketch with all roller-furling sails would be the lazy man's delight.

Yawls were popular at a certain stage of the ocean racing rules, when they were given certain advantages in unpenalized sail area by the way the rule was written. Since that was an era when racing boats also cruised, many yawls could be seen in cruising areas, but the rig really does not recommend itself to the cruising yachtsman. The mizzen is too small to be helpful for anything but a few staysails downwind, and it is just an added expense and collection of equipment that needs maintenance.

Schooners were popular in the early days of cruising, mainly because the yachts were adaptations of commercial coasters and fishing boats, and most of those were schooners. The schooner rig is a great one for speed off the wind, and there is nothing quite as exciting as a broad reach in a schooner when the breeze is fresh. Traditionalists and romantics stick to the schooner out of nostalgia and a love of the special sailing qualities, but the rig is really not a good one for cruising because of difficulty in sail handling (and maintenance). Also, it is not an efficient rig to windward. Despite all this, it is good that some people stick to schooners—they add a picturesque touch to any seascape they grace.

Along with schooners, such character craft as Friendship Sloops,

Chesapeake bugeyes, skipjacks, and even Chinese junks are occasionally glimpsed on the cruising scene. The gaff-rigged, clipper-bowed Friendships, originally Maine workboats of twenty-five to forty feet and named for the town in which they were built, gained popularity as yachts during the Depression of the thirties, when many of them came on the market because they had been outmoded by powerboats, and they could be picked up very cheaply. They sailed well and were very able, if a bit heavy, and gained an ardent band of admirers who perpetuate the type with a special organization. Replicas in fiberglass have also been built.

The Chesapeake boats, with their low, broad hulls and raking masts, were also workboat adaptations that could be bought cheaply, and they too have received fanatic devotion from their admirers, but they are not being replaced by modern replicas.

Power Plants

The question of auxiliary power for cruising sailboats boils down to two choices: inboard versus outboard, and gasoline versus diesel. The first is largely a matter of size of boat, and the latter depends on owner preference. Under thirty feet, outboards can be seriously considered, and below twenty-six feet the decision becomes almost automatic, as most of the stock boats in that range are planned with outboard power in mind. Also, it is easier to trail an outboard-equipped boat.

Sailboat hulls are easily driven, and low-powered outboards in the 9.5-horsepower range or lower have plenty of the oomph needed to push them as fast as they will go. Since this is so, owners of boats that can logically be powered by outboards should recognize the many advantages gained from this type of power. The first is lower cost. An inboard engine is more expensive than an outboard, and the installation costs add even more. Secondly, an inboard takes up more interior space, which is important in a small cruising boat.

Third, an outboard is safer than a gasoline inboard: there is no interior fuel system that could possibly leak into the bilge and set up the ingredients of an explosion. Other advantages are ease of servicing, reliability, and freedom from heat and odor inside the boat.

Since outboards are portable, they can be taken to a service shop rather than having a mechanic come aboard, and an outboard is usually more reliable in starting and operation than a more complicated and sophisticated inboard that has lain idle in the inhospitably damp and humid atmosphere of a closed-up boat.

In boats from twenty-six feet or so on up, it is worthwhile to consider an inboard. Here the power available becomes more important, and outboards bigger than 10 horsepower become ungainly and awkward when they must be wrestled on and off the transom. An inboard, with its more easily accessible controls, can be operated more comfortably. Also, fuel consumption is lower in four-cycle inboards than in the bigger models of two-cycle outboards, where lube oil must be mixed with the fuel. With proper installation and soundproofing, inboards might also be quieter, although great strides have been made in silencing outboards.

Outboards have become so popular and prevalent in the day sailer and small cruising boat categories that motors specially engineered for sailboat use, with more efficient gear ratio for low speeds, long shafts, and bigger propellers, have come on the market. The problem then remains as to whether the motor should be mounted on a transom bracket or in a well. A bracket takes less space away from the cockpit, and ingenious designs of brackets that raise and lower easily to keep the motor out of the water while sailing and put it back in quickly when needed have taken away the disadvantage of having to wrestle the motor over the transom every time it was to be used or stowed. In addition to taking up cockpit space, wells require efficient ventilation and some method of keeping the water from sloshing up around the motor, but the motor can be left there in a permanent installation and need not be handled very often.

The gasoline-versus-diesel question relates strictly to inboards;

diesel outboards have not been available. There are several models of gasoline inboards that have been engineered especially for cruising auxiliaries, with the 25-horsepower range the most popular. Initial cost is the major plus for gasoline; weight per horsepower is better, and in some areas, parts and servicing may be easier to come by. In general, however, diesels make a great deal of sense as auxiliaries for cruising sailboats despite their higher cost and heavier weight-to-horsepower ratio. The latter has been reduced in recent years, and diesel fuel and servicing are almost as readily available as for gasoline engines. The biggest plus for diesels is in safety: the danger from gasoline fumes in the bilge is real in inboards with this type of power. In them, great care must be taken at all times to make sure that there has been no leakage and that the bilge is free. A blower and a bilge alarm are important pieces of equipment with gasoline installations.

Diesels may be a bit harder to start in cold weather, but they are less temperamental about being left idle for long periods of time, which usually happens with so many auxiliary motors. In a cruising boat, the slight extra weight is not a significant factor, though it might be in an ocean racer. One other objection to diesels is the smell of the fuel, which takes getting used to, although it isn't as noticeable in an auxiliary as in a large powerboat with diesel power.

In general, the best advice for cruising sailboats is: outboards to twenty-six feet, diesel inboards above that.

Layout and Accommodations

There are almost as many ways to combine bunks, head, and galley in cruising sailboats as there are boats. It is truly phenomenal how many variations are possible, and the bigger the boat, the greater the opportunity. In a little twenty-two-foot overnighter, there is just so much that can be done in designing the interior arrangements. A couple of V-berths extending into the bow, with the galley area and a head aft of that, is pretty standard, though ingenious things can be done with quarter berths—berths extending aft from the cabin under

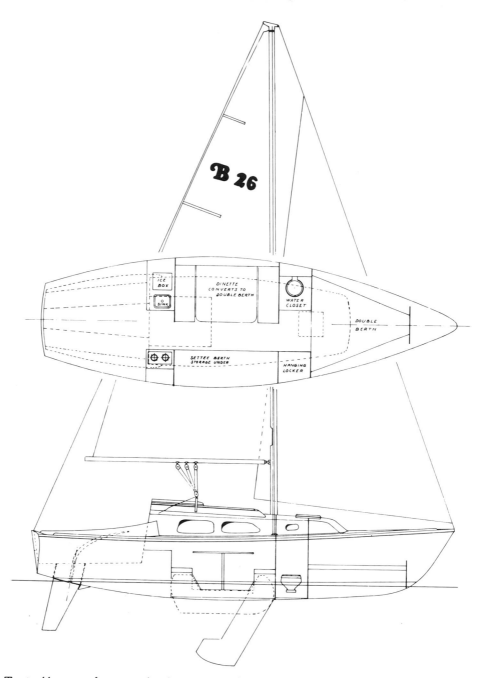

Typical layout of a swing-keel twenty-six-foot trailable, a Balboa 26

the cockpit seats, and dual-purpose use of a space via hideaway galley units, ice chests with chart tables on top, and other such compromises. *Compromise* is the dominant word in discussing cabin layouts. To get one feature, something must be sacrificed in another area, and it is simply a question of balancing out priorities.

We have already gone into sensible capacity guidelines for the number of bunks, and that is, again, very important. If a boat can sleep five or six people, but they cannot get out of the sack without pushing and shoving each other around a dual-purpose area where someone is supposed to be getting breakfast, and it takes half an hour to get one's turn in the head, the five-sleeper arrangement loses some of its charm.

There are momentous problems to decide. Should the galley be near the main hatch so that the cook can remain in social contact with the cockpit, or should it be farther forward so that no one coming down the main companionway puts his foot in the soup as it is being dished out? There is never total agreement on this among boat-buyers, so both layouts are seen with frequency. Should the cabin have a spacious, open feeling, or should it be compartmented off for maximum privacy? When a mixed group is cruising, the latter gains greatly in importance.

In boats up to twenty-six or twenty-eight feet, headroom presents a problem. Sometimes the designer is able to achieve a nice compromise without making the boat look ungainly, and other dodges can be used. Convertible hoods were an early solution, but these have largely been replaced by pop-tops or oversized hatches that fold out and up to make a form of doghouse with full headroom. In the pop-top concept, the cabin roof is raised like a card table on adjustable supports, and curtains or screens are used to fill in the sides if necessary. Headroom is extremely important in smaller boats, especially if more than a weekend is to be spent aboard, and solutions like these are necessary.

A type of layout that was adapted for auxiliaries from the power cruiser field became very popular in boats designed especially for bareboat chartering, and the idea spread to stock boats for private use. That is the tri-cabin layout, which is possible in boats from about thirty-two feet on up and really presents all sorts of possibilities from about thirty-five feet up. In it, the cockpit is located just aft of amidships, roughly under the main boom, with the engine under it, and there is a separate stateroom aft, with its own head. Forward of the cockpit is a main cabin with galley and convertible dinette, or some other form of combining day use and sleeping in one cabin, with a separate cabin forward and a head between these two cabins. The layout is ideal, providing maximum privacy, for two couples and works well enough for six people from about forty feet up, though it is possible for six to use it in smaller sizes. There are infinite variations on the tri-cabin arrangement. One feature that many owners demand is a walk-through passageway from the after cabin to the main cabin. That is nice in nasty weather, but it usually takes away from the engine-room space and sometimes the cockpit layout. Access to the engine and room to work on it are vitally important, which few owners realize until they have to turn themselves into a pretzel to get at the motor in an emergency. Some designs take this into account, but others do not, and it is a point that new buyers often overlook.

Another lack in many stock full-cruising boats, especially those with tri-cabin layouts that are extremely comfortable for sleeping at anchor or in a marina, is of berths that are comfortable and safe during a passage in rough water. If a boat is to be taken on open-water passages, the problem should be considered.

Some other items should be considered in a good cruising boat. Especially helpful is the practice of stowing a plow anchor in a special fitting at the bow, where it can be pulled up and snugged tight without wrestling it, and its load of mud, over the lifelines and onto the deck. That is another split between cruising and racing: so much weight would be a great mistake in the bow of an ocean racer.

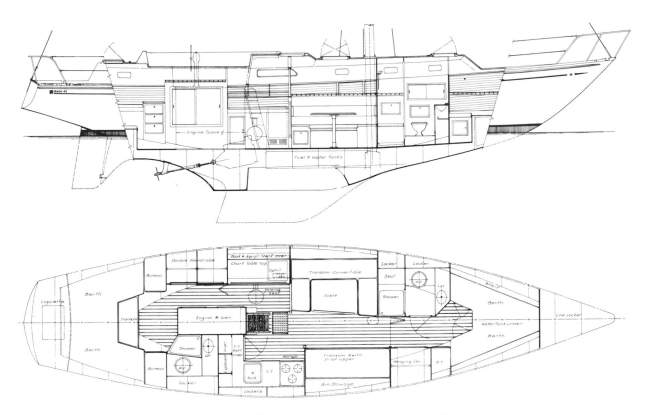

The tri-cabin layout of an Irwin 45 with center cockpit and walk-through passage-way from aft cabin

On full-cruising boats, the boom is often kept high enough over the cockpit so that a Bimini top can be rigged while the boat is under sail. That may look peculiar, and it is an odd experience to sail a boat without being able to look directly up at the sails, but it is a great boon in hot weather, especially down south where the sun is direct and hot.

___14

The How To of Cruising and Chartering

FROM the previous chapter it is obvious that there are a great many variations in cruising boats and a great many ways to cruise. A few people want to round Cape Horn solo, but many more want to fit in some pleasant time afloat within the normal span of their vacation. This chapter is for them.

One succinct piece of advice covers much territory and has already been applied to day sailing: don't do too much. Don't even try to do too much. A shorter itinerary than the maximum that seems possible, shorter days' runs, and a leisurely approach to the whole project will return enormous dividends in relaxation and pleasure. There may be days when there is no alternative to a hard thrash from sunup to sunset so that subsequent days can be relaxed and easy, but they should be the exception. A few of them bring a sense of challenges met and of real accomplishment, but too many foster fatigue and an unpleasant sense of urgency, and these are contrary to the whole philosophy of cruising.

A leisurely start after breakfast, with the dishes washed and everybody "in all respects rady for sea," sets the proper tone for a day of cruising. Arrival in port well before suppertime, with good light, and plenty of time to choose an anchorage and perhaps do errands ashore, ends a day on a relaxing note. It isn't whether you make thirty or sixty miles on a cruise, but the quality of those miles, that is important.

Proper equipment is vital to cruising success. A cruising boat must be a complete living unit afloat. Certain makeshifts and some contrasts to the routines of home are naturally necessary, but it is a mistake to skimp on equipment and to do without whatever amenities the boat can logically provide. A typical list of the equipment a cruising auxiliary of thirty to forty feet should carry is at the end of this chapter. It might seem a bit overwhelming at first impact, but every item on it can make a difference in the quality of life aboard. You are virtually setting up another household, albeit a watery one. Make it a place you are happy to live in.

Electronics

What to do about electronics is another question. Depending on the size of boat, electronic equipment can be important in safety and convenience, but many cruising people would rather keep it at a minimum and avoid the initial expense, plus maintenance woes. Every boat should have a radio to receive weather reports, and few cruising boats operate without some form of transmitter, whether it be VHF for local transmissions or Single Side Band for long-range activity. The latter is advisable for offshore operations and cruises to distant waters, but the initial expense is high. Regulations on radio use change on occasion, and it has been difficult for owners to keep up with the requirements. VHF sets are limited to line-of-sight reception and transmission, which means an effective reception of up to sixty miles from shore stations, and a sending range of something less, depending on the height above water of the equipment. Coast Guard vessels and shore stations monitor and transmit on VHF in their dealings with pleasure craft.

From there on out, the sky's the limit on electronics. Owners who are gadgeteers (and rich) can run the gamut, but the boat must have a power supply sufficient to operate all the equipment, and maintenance in a marine atmosphere is always a problem. There is an old maritime form of Murphy's Law that says that the more stuff you have aboard, the more there is to get out of order.

After a radio, the next most important item is probably a depth sounder, which is an easily used and very important aid in piloting, especially in fog or at night. A radio direction finder is also a near-must, but it can be combined with a radio receiver in a simplified form that is helpful in emergencies and for routine checks. More sophisticated—and expensive—items like radar, Loran, and Omni are very helpful in piloting and navigation, but thousands of cruising sailors get along without them. For coastal work, radar is probably the most important of these.

Gadgets like water-makers, water-pressure systems, deep freezes, air conditioners, microwave ovens, shore converters, and mechanical refrigeration can make life pleasant if you can afford them, but you will soon be in a category of needing a resident electrical engineer to keep everything working. Most of that gear is for the larger, more elaborate yachts with professional crews. In this group, the Number 1 vote goes to water-pressure systems and shore converters.

One item that does make sense if you intend to go offshore at all is an emergency position indicating radio beacon (EPIRB) that can send out a distress signal to aid search and rescue planes and vessels. Originally developed for aircraft, it has been made available for pleasure boats.

Ocean racing sailboats load up with all sorts of electronic gadgets that tell apparent wind angle, wind velocity, speed through the water, and water temperature. These, again, can be pleasantly helpful while cruising, but they really aren't that necessary on a nonracing boat.

Probably the most important would be some form of knot meter as an aid in dead reckoning.

Unless you are a dyed-in-the-wool gadgeteer and really know and enjoy electronics and their workings, you can end up being a slave to them on a cruising boat.

Dinghies

What to do about a dinghy? That is always a problem, and it becomes increasingly larger as the size of the cruising boat gets smaller. A dinghy is a necessity in most cruising areas, and the only way to avoid the need for one is to spend every night at a marina. At the present rate of docking charges, you could soon pay for a dinghy by avoiding the price of just a few marina visits.

Towing a dinghy is a good solution, and most of the bareboat charter yachts in southern waters follow this practice. They have roomy, able dinghies that tow well—boats with a good lift to their bow sections and a broad section aft, with enough deadrise to give them lateral and directional stability, and it is remarkable how well they

Dinghies are an important adjunct to cruising. Correct anchoring allows cruising yachtsmen to relax and enjoy themselves

handle good-sized seas with a minimum of fuss. Many owners prefer not to tow, however, because of the drag a dinghy adds and to avoid the rare time when the dinghy does swamp or become otherwise unmanageable. Stowage aboard then calls for some ingenuity.

Some boats have davits at the stern for carrying the dinghy. This does solve the problem of space on board, and the dinghy is also easy to handle. The rig looks ungainly in even the larger boats over forty feet, and there is a more serious drawback if any offshore work is contemplated. A following sea could "poop" the dinghy, filling it and tearing it, and probably the davits, loose, with a real potential for ripping up the deck as well. For coastwise work davits are a possible solution, the more so the bigger the boat gets, but then there is probably more room on deck too.

Deck stowage across the foredeck, across the transom, or on the cabin trunk is often seen but always presents the problem of wrestling the dink aboard, unless it is a tiny one. Some owners have worked out ingenious solutions of cutaway doghouses of which the dinghy becomes a part when stowed, and halyards can be used for hoisting heavier dinghies aboard.

An increasingly popular answer to the dinghy problem is to use an inflatable. Rubber-like synthetics have been developed that are extremely tough and snag-, tear-, and abrasion-resistant. Inflatables come in all sizes from little play toys for the junior set to big assault boats for half a platoon. The six-man size that can be powered by an outboard or rowed is a good choice for medium-sized cruising boats, for it can be stowed in little more than the space a big fender takes up when deflated. They are a bit skittish for towing because of their flat bottoms, and some skippers bring them right up hard against the after pulpit, with the bow made fast there and just the stern in the water. That is all right in smooth water, but not in a sea. Most boats over thirty feet have room to lash them across the transom or on top of the cabin in a tri-cabin boat, or forward of the mast. Inflatables are light enough to make launching and bringing aboard easy.

Galleys

The galley is a very special department. It is of prime importance in cruising, as an angry or uncomfortable cook can spoil the fun for everybody. Location has been touched on in the previous chapter, and most cooks prefer a galley that keeps them in contact with the rest of the crew while meals are being prepared, rather than isolating them forward. There should still be freedom of movement around the galley area, if possible, so the cook isn't being elbowed while in the middle of mixing something. A galley along one side of the main cabin, with a dinette opposite, has worked out well for these reasons, especially in the kind of cruising in which the boat makes port every night.

For those contemplating longer passages at sea, an L- or U-shaped galley, where the cook can wedge in tightly, perhaps with a safety belt on, is much easier to work in and much safer, and everything is within easy reach. It makes cooking more of a one-person job, whereas the cook can more easily have helpers in the kind of galley that runs along the bulkhead. If the boat is big enough to have a professional cook, the galley should be located forward of the main cabin, where the cook can work without disturbing, or being disturbed by, the socializing of the owner's party.

Stowage for food, utensils, crockery, and pots and pans must be carefully thought out and not skimped. Special dish and glass racks that make the most use of available space are helpful. Modern plastics have produced dishes, cups, and glasses that look and feel like china but are unbreakable, a real boon on a boat. Liberal use of disposable skillets, foil, paper towels, and also paper plates and plastic glasses can lighten the load in the galley.

Fuel for the stove is another item that causes considerable discussion and disagreement in cruising ranks. Electricity is only possible in the biggest luxury yachts with the generating equipment to supply the juice. It is clean and efficient, but not widely used. For most boats it comes down to bottled gas versus alcohol, and the latter is more popular.

Every system has its booby traps, and safety requirements must be rigidly adhered to. Gas is simple, clean, and quick, but it is also the most lethal, because of the possibility of explosion. For that reason, insurance requirements stipulate that the bottles must be stored on deck in their own vented box or compartment. In smaller boats, that presents a space problem, and bottled gas is therefore found more often in larger craft. In Europe, where insurance regulations are different, many small cruising sailboats are equipped with camper-type stoves which have bottled gas cylinders attached directly to the stove. In the type of installation required in the United States, the shut-off valve must be turned off at all times when the equipment is not in use; proper procedures on this should be followed very carefully.

Alcohol is the most widely used stove fuel, with kerosene and solid fuels also fairly common. Alcohol is pressurized so that it sprays out of a nozzle into a preheated burner as a vapor, and once it lights properly it makes a good flame. The problems with alcohol are in achieving the right pressure and in making sure that unvaporized liquid doesn't flow into the burners, which can cause a quick and dangerous flare-up.

Steps for priming and lighting must be followed carefully. First, with the shut-off valve closed, pump up pressure in the alcohol tank to the desired indication on the pressure dial. Then open the shut-off valve. Next, release about one tablespoonful of alcohol into the burner cup by a quick opening and closing of the burner valve. Light the alcohol in the cup as a primer to heat the burner. When the primer flame has just burned out, reopen the burner valve and light the vapor that should come out if the right amount of pressure has been pumped. If this has been done right, the alcohol comes out vaporized and lights like a gas flame. If it sputters or gurgles, there is not enough vapor, and priming must be done over. If the burner valve is not turned off between preheating and lighting the vapor, too much liquid can collect in the burner, and it will flare up into a roaring pyre very quickly. If that happens, turn off the shut-off valve immediately; it should be located where access is not blocked by a burner flare-up. Placing it behind the stove is a serious mistake. Alcohol fires can be safely doused with water if a flare-up occurs.

Solid fuels, such as Sterno, are safest and easiest, but they do not produce as hot a flame as other fuels, and cooking must be confined to heating up stews, hashes, and canned vegetables. An adapter that concentrates the flame helps the efficiency of solid fuels. Many boats carry a single-burner gimbaled Sterno stove that swings on a bulkhead fitting to supplement the regular stove for boiling water, heating soup, or warming a one-dish meal when underway in rough weather.

Clothing and Luggage

Life aboard a cruising boat gains greatly in comfort and quality if clothing and luggage are sensibly handled. Almost without fail, everyone brings too much aboard in the way of clothing, and anything but soft, collapsible luggage should be taboo. Duffle bags are the perfect solution—they are roomy, light, and easily stowed. Nonskid shoes, not just any old sneakers, are an absolute must.

Clothing should be durable, comfortable, and easily washed. Normally it can be worn longer on a boat than onshore, since it doesn't get as dirty, and standards can be relaxed with no harm done. In areas of changeable weather, good sweaters and windbreakers are vital. A warm, calm summer morning can turn into a raw afternoon on even the hottest day if a sea breeze makes up. A windbreaker, even a light one, over a sweater is a good combination for cutting down chill factor.

There is excellent foul-weather gear now on the market from a number of suppliers, from light, pliable stuff to the heavy-duty fisherman type, and the kind of sailing to be done governs the choice.

Nonskid boots, a must, should be kept aboard to avoid fouling the tread with shore dirt. A place to hang wet foul-weather gear without affecting the whole below-deck area is important. If the boat isn't big enough for a special locker, the head might be a likely place.

As in everything else to do with a cruising boat, keep it as simple as possible.

Anchoring

One of the keys to successful cruising is correct anchoring. Many a night that should have been restful and secure has been ruined by a dragging anchor or by boats, anchored too close to each other, banging together when the wind or tide changes. There is no great mystique to anchoring, but many otherwise-competent sailors seem to have blind spots on the subject.

The equipment comes first. Four types of anchors are seen fairly often. First is the yachtsman's anchor, the regular old-fashioned one of conventional illustrations, which is not much used by yachtsmen any more because it is cumbersome and awkward to handle. Holding power-to-weight ratio is not particularly good, and stowage can also be a problem. If a heavy enough anchor is used, the holding properties are good, but it is likely to foul the anchor line if the vessel swings much, since one fluke extends above the bottom while the anchor is digging in.

The Northill anchor, originally developed for seaplanes, folds compactly for stowage and has good holding properties in relation to weight, but it has the same general configuration as the old-fashioned anchor when dug in and is therefore subject to having the exposed fluke fouled in the same manner.

Extremely popular for all sizes of cruising boat is the Danforth anchor, which stows flat and has two triangular flukes that both dig in when the anchor is on the bottom. Once properly set, the Danforth has remarkable holding properties for its size and weight, and it is available in sizes from tiny three-pound dinghy anchors to walloping big ones for maxi yachts. *Danforth* was the trade name for a patented anchor, but the patent has run out, and many other manufacturers now market close variations of the original patented design. Danforths are excellent for light lunch hooks and for great security and reliability for one-directional pull. If the boat swings and starts pulling in the other direction, the Danforth tends to pop out, rather than slue around while holding, as other anchors do, and if the boat starts making leeway too fast, it may skip over the bottom without digging in again. Another Danforth quirk is that it is easily fouled if a shell, beer can, or other hard object jams between the flukes or becomes impaled on one.

For small boats, Danforths make great sense because of their light weight and ease of handling and stowing. They are excellent lunch hooks and spare anchors on bigger boats.

For cruising, the plow anchor has long been popular as a type—it has good holding properties in a variety of bottoms—but it was always hard to stow and to handle on deck. That problem disappeared with the development of the bow chock, into which a plow seats perfectly, so that it does not have to be wrestled onto the deck. This type of installation has become widespread on cruising auxiliaries. The plow's only troublesome characteristic is that it does not hold very well in a soft bottom, but drags very slowly, so imperceptibly that it might not be noticed for quite some time unless a careful continuous check was being taken. It is also no better than any other type on a hard, grassy bottom, the worst kind of holding ground.

Nylon rope is a must as anchor-rode material, and it greatly enhances the holding power of any anchor to have a shot of chain as the last few feet of the rode. Marine chandleries usually have charts that show the size of rope needed, and the weight of anchor, for given sizes and types of boats.

Once the proper equipment is aboard, it should then be handled correctly, or it could still fail. Giving proper scope is all-important, with 6 to 1 (scope-to-depth of water) a fairly good general rule of thumb. Conditions create expectations; a small Danforth can hold a remarkably large yacht if it is given two or three times the normal scope.

Letting go under control, with the vessel just beginning to fall back slightly—rather than a shotputter's heave with a tangle of flukes and line as the boat continues to move forward across the intended location for the anchor when it hits bottom—gives a much better chance for the anchor to hold. With the boat falling back slowly, the anchor line should be snubbed, setting the anchor, a bit before the ultimately desired scope is out. If the rode snubs up taut and the vessel stops her backward slide and begins to ride in one place like a captive pendulum, the line can then be let out the rest of the way to the desired depth. If there is doubt about how to gauge the amount of line to let out, it can be marked with bits of colored cloth, or some other signs, at known intervals.

Pick a range on shore—a tree and a house, two flagpoles, and prominent objects that line up on each other—and keep checking the range as the boat rides. Be sure you have left enough room for a 360° swing around the anchor's location at the scope that is out without hitting another boat. This can be quite a problem in some crowded, popular harbor like Cuttyhunk on a weekend evening. Catalina, as the only convenient weekending target for the thousands of boats based in the Los Angeles area, has almost no anchoring spots that can be selected by the skipper. Permanently installed strings of moorings, controlled by various clubs and organizations, fill almost every cove.

Piloting

Whole books have been written on piloting, and the only intent here is to give some general hints. Procedures should be studied and known, and then there is no real difficulty in successful coastwise piloting for someone familiar with the compass, charts, dividers, and parallel rulers (or the various patented substitutes).

The Number 1 must in good piloting is to know at all times where you are in even the most beautiful and least threatening weather. Always check the nearest buoy for its identification, as well as landmarks on shore, lighthouses, and other charted features. Check out course and speed between known objects for any inconsistencies that could cause trouble later. Never assume a position without checking it, unless you have nothing but assumptions to go on. Doing all that in good weather builds a familiarity with the boat that is helpful if fog sets in.

Make use of all available publications. In addition to government tide, current, and light lists, excellent commercially published yachtsmen's cruising guides for every popular area are generally available in marine supply stores. These are updated annually for such areas as the Bahamas, the intracoastal waterway, New England, and the Pacific Coast, and there are also hardcover guides of a more permanent nature on most of the popular areas. The government Small Craft Chart series also contains a great amount of helpful cruising information on each chart. Continuing study of guides and charts provides a wealth of fascinating information that not only aids in piloting but also makes the cruise more interesting.

As mentioned before, the two electronic aids that are most helpful in piloting are a depth sounder and a radio direction finder. Use of them in good weather as a check pays dividends in poor visibility. Confidence in your ability to use and interpret them is reassuring in fog or at night.

Fog is the bane of the cruising yachtsman, but its terrors can be reduced through this sort of confidence. In addition to exact figuring of course, speed, and current factors, other senses lend help when the eyes are relatively useless. Sound, though it does play tricks in fog, helps locate whistlers, bell buoys, and lighthouse hooters, as well as waves lapping on a beach or breaking against rocks, or even the chirping of birds.

In the same way, the aroma of pine trees, bayberry, or a seaweedy beach warns of the proximity of land. Less romantically, industrial odors, smoke, or automobile smells sometimes tell a story in built-up areas. Keeping track of wind direction is often an important element of fog navigation. All of this is sometimes called *barking dog* navigation, so named because Maine fishermen often used to find their way home by listening for the familiar noise of a neighborhood dog.

Piloting is important for safety, but it is also one of the more rewarding challenges of cruising and an integral part of it.

Chartering

Every cruising yachtsman dreams of far horizons, of landfalls in the Caribbean or South Pacific, and of curving white beaches under a stand of palms, but few have the time, or the type of boat, to take them there. There is a substitute, though: chartering. As long as there have been yachts, owners have, on occasion, placed their beloved craft on charter to help meet expenses. For many years, this was all

A rail-down passage in the Virgin Islands, one of the joys of southern chartering

on an individual basis, with the boat intended primarily for the owner's use and only secondarily for charter. Direct negotiation through classified ads, or with a yacht broker in the picture, was the method of handling a charter; there was no real organization to the practice.

With the coming of the jet age, however, and the greatly expanded mobility made possible through it, chartering in distant areas became a viable possibility. A whole new industry grew up, gathering steam through the sixties. Boats were put into service as full-time charter yachts, set up solely for this purpose as commercial ventures. First came professionally crewed yachts, many of them older vessels with their glory days behind them but still roomy and comfortable. The first ones were based in English Harbour, Antigua, and soon after that in the Bahamas and Virgin Islands. By 1960, there were perhaps two or three dozen boats in full-time charter service spread through these three areas. There were also a few yachts in various parts of the Mediterranean.

The charter party would be guests aboard, with no more responsibility for operating the vessel than guests in a hotel, unless they happened to feel like steering or trimming a sheet. Professional cooks (or perhaps the skipper's family) would take care of all galley and housekeeping duties. Experienced yachtsmen enjoyed the chance to see new areas, and inexperienced ones enjoyed the security of a professional crew. That type of operation is still very much alive in all these areas, and as trade increased, some yachts were designed and built especially for the service.

Many boat owners who experienced such a cruise longed to command a vessel in exotic surroundings rather than lolling as pampered guests of a professional crew. Few could bring their own boats so far, and pressures eventually developed for establishing a new kind of chartering: bareboat. There was nothing new about the practice of experienced sailors taking over someone else's boat, but it had never been set up with boats intended exclusively for the service,

A modern crewed charter yacht, a fifty-three-foot fiberglass ketch, moored at St. Lucia's Pitons, a highlight of the Caribbean

as opposed to privately owned boats that were occasionally offered for charter. From small beginnings in the late sixties, commercially operated charter fleets grew; by 1975 there were approximately 270 boats available for full-time bareboating in Florida, the Bahamas, the Virgins, and the Lesser Antilles; the practice had spread to Scandinavia and the Aegean as well. In 1974, over 31,000 people took part in bareboat chartering in American-operated yachts in the major areas.

Bareboating is usually in smaller boats of twenty-five to forty-five feet, as opposed to forty feet on up for professionally crewed boats, with most of these in at least the sixty-foot range. Most of the boats have been designed for bareboating, and that is where the center-cockpit, tri-cabin layout first became popular. Costs are lower in bareboating, but the charter party must do all its own work of operating the boat, cooking, cleaning up, and housekeeping. To make the job easier, most of the charter services stock the boats ahead of time with standard menus and the charterer's liquor order sent in advance. Everything is scientifically organized so that briefing sessions on local navigation and on operation of the boat take less than half a day. Charterers must satisfy the charter company that they are competent to operate the boat, via a résumé, references, and possibly a check-out aboard a boat on the scene. Anybody who can pay the bill, however, can qualify to take a professionally crewed charter cruise.

In general, prices on the latter match the daily rates at luxury resorts or cruise ships, with the advantage that there are no extras while aboard. Bareboating prices correspond to the rates of the more informal, though first-class, clubbier island resorts; again, no extras.

Do's and don't's are similar to those for cruising in your own boat. Don't do too much. Relax and enjoy the new surroundings, particularly because of the shock to the system of the quick switch from northern winter to tropical climes. Keep clothing light and practical and use soft, stowable luggage. Everyone always brings too much. Be very careful, without fail, about sunburn. Direct rays of a tropical sun burn like no northern sun ever did.

Arranging a charter can be simple. The boating magazines are full

A fleet of bareboats ready for charter at Somes Sound, Mount Desert Island, Maine

of charter company ads and ads for professionally crewed boats, and most of them have agents in the continental United States. In making an inquiry, gives as much information as possible about the makeup of your party, sailing experience (very specific for bareboating), special interests—such as diving or fishing—and price range. Most of the agencies will book the entire trip as a package, including air transportation and ground connections in the charter area.

Commercial chartering has brought those far horizons much closer and opened them to many an erstwhile armchair dreamer. The next chapter will go into the general characteristics of the popular cruising areas.

RECOMMENDED EQUIPMENT LIST FOR CRUISING BOATS

Anchor rodes, 150', 5/8" Nylon, 2
Anchors
Ammeter
Anemometer, pocket
Ashtrays, beanbag
Awning, Dacron, cockpit
Batteries, 2 sets of 2, 12 V
Battery, switch
Bilge pump, hand
Binoculars, 7 x 50
Blankets, Dacron for all bunks
Boat hook
Bow chock, mahogany, and roller for
    anchor
Brushes
   Long-handled
   Scrub
   Whisk broom
Chafing gear on lines
Charcoal grill
Clothes hangers
Clothespins
Compass
Courtesy flag

Cushions, cockpit
Cushions, life preserver, 4-6
Dishcloths, 2
Dish locker
Dock lines
Dynaplates
Electric bonding system
Fenders
Fire extinguisher
First-aid kit
Fishing rods, reels, and line
Flares, hand, emergency
Flashlights, 3
Flippers, masks, and snorkels
Fly-swatter
Fog bell
Fuel filter
Fuel measuring stick
Funnel, fuel, with strainer
Funnel, water
Galley equipment
   Beer-can opener, stainless steel
   Butter box and cover
   Chore Girls

Coffeepot
Corkscrew
Double boiler and lid
Frying pan
Funnel, plastic
Glasses
Ice pick
Insulated glasses, coffee, 6
Juice container and top, 36-oz.
Juice container and top, 50-oz.
Juice squeezer
Knife, large
Knives, paring, 2
Plates 8", 6
Plates 10", 6
Soup bowls, 6
Mixing bowls, large
Mixing bowls, small
Peeler
Potholders, 2
Sponges, cellulose, 2; galley, 2
Sugar bowl
Tableware, 6 each knives, forks,
   teaspoons, tablespoons,
   stainless steel
Toaster
Turner
Utensil box
Genoa sheet gear, including track and
   fair-lead blocks
Ice bag
Insect repellent
International navigation lights
Jerry jugs for extra water
Lead line
Life preservers, horseshoe and bracket
Light bulbs, extra
Lightning grounding system

Mattresses, seat cushions on each bunk
Mirror, head
Mooring cleats
Mop, cellulose
Navigation gear
   Necessary charts
   Dividers
   Parallel rulers
   Pencils
Oars and oarlocks for skiff
Oil-pressure gauge
Outboard motor on skiff
Pillowcases
Pillows, foam
Radiotelephone
Roller-furling gear for jib
Roller reefing, main boom
Screens
Scuppers (through-deck)
Sheets for berths
Signal horn
Skiff
Stern pole and ensign
Strainer, fuel
Swimming ladder
Tool kit
   Extra fuses
   Nuts and bolts
   Nylon cord
   Plastic tape
   Tool set
Towels, supply of large and medium
Tow rope, ½" polypropylene, for skiff
Valves, fuel shut-off
Ventilators, engine-room to meet CG
   requirements
Washcloths
Wind scoop, Dacron on forward hatch
   for hyperventilation

_____15

Cruising Areas

AS A fortunate complement to the growing popularity of cruising in the whole boating spectrum, North America is blessed with a wealth of fine cruising areas. Not too long ago, the cruising yachtsman was confined to the waters of home, or at least those that could be reached from home in normal vacation time. Before the jet age, only the very wealthy and the retired could manage to range through the various, and highly varied, cruising areas that take in Penobscot Bay and Puget Sound, the Bahamas and Baja California, Buzzards Bay and Biscayne Bay, Georgian Bay and the Grenadines, to name a few. Now, with swift air travel and the availability of charter boats, horizons are wider, and every cruising devotee can dream of distant areas with at least a fair possibility that the dream can come true in the normal course of events.

It is no longer unusual for a Chicagoan to know Nantucket and Friday Harbor well, or a New Yorker to be familiar with Sir Francis Drake Channel, the North Channel, and Mount Desert Island. And such is the spread of cruising areas that the most dedicated adventurer could spend every vacation for years sampling a different one without worrying about duplication. West Coast sailors jet to the

Caribbean for winter cruising, Easterners go west, and Midwesterners spread out in all directions.

Here, in a swing starting from the Northeast, is a rundown of the best cruising areas and their special characteristics.

Nova Scotia

A few rugged individualists, unsatisfied by the tamer waters of the Northeast United States, venture far to the north and east, to Newfoundland, Labrador, and Greenland, but they are exceptional adventurers in the tradition of explorers of old. In the same direction, but closer to home and more easily accessible and manageable in the scope of normal vacations, is Canada's Nova Scotian peninsula, a land of quick summer, fog, strong winds, and lovely rolling countryside backing picturesque fishing hamlets. Big ports like Yarmouth, Halifax, and Sydney offer civilized contrasts, and the most popular cruising area is the Bras d'Or Lakes, an inland system on Cape Breton Island, the northern half of Nova Scotia. Away from the harsh northern seas and protected by the land around it, the system of connected lakes basks in a warm climate amid some of the loveliest scenery anywhere, with many peaceful anchorages. It is a long pull for American boats to get there, but well worth it, and charter services have recently developed to cater to visitors who do not have the time to make it in their own boats.

Maine

Many yachtsmen are completely happy with their lot as long as they are cruising in Maine. Maine—"Down East" because it is downwind from Boston in the prevailing summer sou'westers—is unique in its atmosphere and in the number of excellent cruising harbors. On the chart, the coastline has the look of the torn hem of a skirt. From Casco Bay eastward, it doesn't have a straight line on it.

Maine offers rocky shorelines, pine trees, and bracing air

Points, capes, and headlands thrust seaward between river mouths, bays, and coves; thousands of islands, from mere rocks to large land masses like Mount Desert (pronounced like the last course of a meal, not a sandy waste), string along the entire length. Behind the first line of islands on the outer coast, a network of rivers, guts, reaches, and thoroughfares permits passage along much of the coast in protected waters deep enough for even the largest yachts. No one yachtsman has ever cruised long enough to anchor in every good harbor in Maine, and that multiple lure brings fanatics back summer after summer. Many also have favorite spots that are so attractive that they bear revisiting time and again.

Along with this oversupply of cruising anchorages, Maine's atmosphere is almost unique in North America—though there are areas of the Great Lakes and Puget Sound that are reminiscent of it. The shores are uniformly rocky and lined with evergreens, and behind them, hills and even good-sized mountains form a graceful backdrop. Much of the coast is wild and unspoiled; harbor after harbor offers perfect isolation in a natural setting. A veteran Maine cruising enthusiast considers a day unusually crowded if he spots half a dozen other cruising yachts and has to share an evening anchorage with other boats.

Along with the beauty of its setting, Maine's climate is vigorously bracing at its best. The air is clean and clear, and the afternoon sea breeze has a special tang in its combination of salt and pine trees. The season is quite short. Most cruising is done in July and August, though June and September are possible months and October has many golden days as the season wanes.

But—and a big one it is—there is also fog.

Anyone cruising in Maine must be prepared to handle fog navigation. There are good summers and bad summers, but even in the good ones, there has to be a reasonable expectancy of some fog, especially early in the summer. The Gulf of Maine is a fog factory because its waters are cold. They are fed by a reverse, south-flowing current from Labrador and Newfoundland and do not feel the influence of the Gulf Stream, which has curved far offshore from the continent by the time it reaches the latitude of Maine. When early-summer heat waves warm up the air over the large land masses west of the Gulf of Maine, and the general flow of weather from west to east moves the warm, humid air out over the cold waters of the Gulf, condensation into instant fog is the result. It comes in quickly, often with very little warning, and is usually heavy and impenetrable. Under "ideal" conditions (for it), fog can stick around for a week or more with very few breaks. On my first cruising venture in Maine, we had eight days of fog and about four hours of sailing, but the inland waterways saved the cruise. Often the fog only fills in over the outer coast, leaving the passages behind the islands fog-free and sunny. We did a lot of powering to get anywhere, but we were seldom fog-bound in harbor and had no idle days when we couldn't move somewhere.

The tide, both in its rise and fall and in the swiftness of its currents, is very much a part of Maine cruising too. The range is great, requiring care in anchoring and in tying alongside piers, and it is important to know the state of the tide at all times. With this great range, and due to the configuration of much of the coast, with narrow passages between islands, and bays and rivers that narrow gradually as they extend inland, the currents are strong and tricky. Typical are two narrow guts known as Upper and Lower Hell Gate on the Sasanoa River that runs between the Kennebec and the Sheepscot. The current, roiling with rips, overfalls, and whirlpools, thrusts through them at close to seven knots.

Fog and current are challenges in Maine cruising, but certainly not deterrents enough to keep anyone away.

The most popular cruising area extends from Casco Bay to the southwest, to the Mount Desert region. Eastward from Mount Desert, the coast is straighter and lonelier, with fewer harbors. Maine veterans will tell you that the experienced cruising skipper always turns to port when coming out of a Maine harbor—in other words, go east no matter where you are to get into better cruising. That purist's view overexaggerates, but the farther east one goes, the wilder, more natural, and more isolated the surroundings are. Marinas, as they are known in the rest of the country, are rather scarce, partly because of the tidal range. Anchoring out is standard procedure, and only a few major centers like Portland (whose yacht harbor is at Falmouth Foreside), Boothbay Harbor, Camden, and Northeast Harbor have extensive facilities. Chartering is possible through several agencies and brokers and a large fleet of "dude cruise" head boats.

Maine enthusiasts look on its drawbacks as stimulating challenges, and all in all, the Maine coast must rank as one of the great cruising areas of the continent.

Southern New England

Not far behind, and in fact preferred by some, is the cruising area centered on Cape Cod and the islands. Between Maine and the Cape, the western shore of Massachusetts Bay supports tremendous local activity in ports like Marblehead, Manchester, Hingham, Cohasset, and the many corners of Boston harbor, but it is not cruising country. Rather, it supplies many of the boats that head Down East to Maine or south of the Cape for their vacation cruising.

The north side of the Cape has relatively few harbors big enough, well-protected enough, or deep enough to attract visitors, but it is a different story once through the canal. Buzzards Bay, Nantucket Sound, Vineyard Sound, Narragansett Bay, and Block Island Sound are lined with excellent harbors that have long been cruising favorites. Their only drawback is that they are so easily within range of major population centers that their most popular harbors have become jammed with boats at the peak of summer activity. The season is a bit longer than in Maine, but much of the activity is still concentrated in July and August. May and June are possible, and September and most of October are really the best. Fog is likely in the earlier months and late-summer-cruising sailors should keep an eye out for hurricanes. They are infrequent, but when they hit, as in 1938, 1944, and 1954, they can devastate the low-lying coast and such funnel-shaped bodies of water as Buzzards and Narragansett bays. Usually there is ample warning of the approach of a tropical disturbance for boats to seek safe shelter.

A quiet anchorage on the south shore of Cape Cod

Tidal currents are strong in constricted waters like the famous race at Woods Hole, and—in contrast to Maine, where one is either bouncing off a rock or safely in deep water—there are many shallow areas. The shoals are mostly sandy, and there are very few rocks, but careful piloting at all times is a must.

Just as the bottom contours are very different from Maine, so is the shore area. It is sand country. Yellow bluffs topped by bayberry and scrub pine, and sand dunes fringed in salt grass, are the normal scenery ashore. There are more towns, closer together, full of atmosphere. Shingled saltbox houses, or the more stately mansions from the prosperous whaling era, set amid towering elms, are a feast of architecture and atmosphere. There are more marinas and boatyards, but all of them, and the anchorage areas, are under tremendous pressure during the height of the summer rush.

Narragansett Bay is a world of its own, with Newport the yachting capital. With a big harbor, several major yards, and first-class marinas—as well as a wealth of sightseeing attractions ashore in historic buildings and the elaborate "cottages" of Newport's heyday as a social center—it is the hub of organized activity such as the America's Cup, the New York Yacht Club cruise, and the start of the Bermuda Race. The bay has many good cruising anchorages, though civilization is close at hand. Block Island, twelve miles off the Rhode Island shore, is a magnet for cruising boats from east, west, and north with a spacious enough harbor to accommodate the biggest influx.

The real heart of the area lies in the islands south of Cape Cod and the surrounding waters. Buzzards Bay is famous for its smoky afternoon sou'wester, one of the most reliable—and brawniest—sailing breezes in the country. The Elizabeth Islands separate the bay from Vineyard Sound and the bigger islands of Martha's Vineyard and Nantucket. Cuttyhunk, at the southwestern end of the Elizabeths, is one of the busiest cruising harbors anywhere at the height of the season. Block Island is the gateway from the west to this area.

Great Salt Pond, Block Island, a popular cruising crossroads

Edgartown on the Vineyard and Nantucket Harbor are the major attractions of the whole area. Edgartown can be overwhelmed by visiting boats, and its shore facilities are very limited, but Nantucket has a mammoth harbor and a large luxury marina on its historic waterfront. The south shore of the Cape is lined with excellent harbors such as Harwichport, Wianno, Falmouth, and Woods Hole.

The summer weather is mild, keyed to the afternoon sou'wester, on the average day, though it is mixed with sparkling nor'westers and rainy nor'easters as a normal pattern.

For those who have no time to bring their own boats into the area, there are several cruise schooners, and many local boats are available through yacht brokers for bareboat charter, though there are no commercially operated fleets of bareboat charter yachts as in southern waters because of the shortness of the season.

Long Island Sound

This inland sea between Long Island and Connecticut, one hundred miles long and two to fifteen miles wide, is ideally set up for small-boat operations. It has dozens of good harbors, especially in its western half, and topnotch facilities in many ports, but it has two serious lacks for the cruising sailor: wind and privacy. More yachts are concentrated in western Long Island Sound than in any other area of the country, and the harbors are chock-a-block. Home-based boats take up so much room that cruising visitors have difficulty finding mooring space, and sailing conditions are poor at the height of the season. The land mass of Long Island, covered with superhighways, shopping centers, and mammoth housing developments, all of which build up a heat barrier in the normally still air of a summer morning, blocks the afternoon sea breeze that hits along the South Shore of Long Island at midday. Often it cannot penetrate to the Sound until late afternoon, if at all, and many Sound days are breathlessly windless, with sailboats slatting in motorboat wakes.

Most sailboats based on the Sound head east for cruising. The Connecticut shore from New Haven east does have attractive anchorages and less crowding in such spots as the Thimble Islands and Duck Island Roads, but better conditions start in the New London area, with Fisher's Island Sound and the eastern tip of Long Island providing many pleasant ports, such as Mystic, Stonington, Fisher's Island West Harbor, Greenport, Dering Harbor, Three Mile Harbor, and Montauk.

All in all, the Sound is best left to its local population. The cruising visitor should look elsewhere.

Chesapeake Bay

Between New York and Chesapeake Bay, the long, straight Jersey Coast, with a handful of inlets leading to tidal flats, supports a great amount of local boating but is not cruising country. Delaware Bay offers less to the cruising yachtsman than almost any other body of water of similar size in the country.

The Chesapeake is another story, however. Like Maine, it has an inexhaustible supply of harbors, a lifetime project and then some for a full-time cruising sailor, but the similarities stop there. Its shores are low, for the most part, either farm country or pine forests, with few hills or bluffs. Although it has many towns and cities, much of it is still undeveloped, especially in the lower half.

The Chesapeake's two-hundred-mile length is fed by an incredible number of tributaries, from big rivers like the Potomac to tiny creeks (half of which seem to be named Mill Creek), and the tributaries have tributaries in an endless skein of waterways. Military installations and Baltimore and its industries occupy the upper Western Shore, but below it, the Magothy River, Annapolis, and the West, South, and Rhode Rivers play host to a tremendous fleet of yachts. Marinas and service facilities abound, but there are so many anchorages that it is still good cruising country. South of the Potomac, the Western Shore has numerous quiet anchorages on the many creeks and small rivers that feed into the main bay. The pace of life slows down to a walk here, and it is easy to find peace and isolation. In fact, it is hard to find anything else all the way to the hustle and bustle of Hampton Roads, dominated by the U.S. Navy and heavy commercial traffic.

And then there is the Eastern Shore. "The Shore," as it is generally referred to on the bay, is a way of life unto itself. Modern civilization has made inroads, but that part of the country has changed less since colonial days than almost any other settled area in the United States. From the Sassafras River on the north all the way to Cape Charles, the Eastern Shore is a watery maze of tributary systems, with the Wye, Chester, Miles, and Choptank rivers, their quiet towns, and attendant creeks, all providing the pleasantest kind of gunkholing. Some centers like Oxford are major yachting installations with dozens of yards and services, but it is still easy, despite the thousands of boats that cruise the Chesapeake, to find a quiet creek or cove in one of the many tributaries. Distances are short all through the bay, and there is never a need for a long hard push to make another harbor.

In the middle of the bay, two fascinating islands, Smith and

The Chesapeake abounds in quiet creeks

Tangier, are unique in their isolation and evocations of times past.

The Chesapeake has a long season, and the climate is mild and pleasant for much of the year. Some locals keep their boats in commission all year and only give up steady operations in December, January, and February. From April through November chances are high for good cruising weather, though there are a few drawbacks. November and April can be blowy and cold, with warm days mixed in, and mid-June to mid-September is a period of light breezes and thunder squalls. Summer heat also brings out the bugs, and no one cruises the Chesapeake without screens. Another bugaboo is the summer jellyfish infestation. The bonus months are May and October. While other areas are still digging out or bundling up, the Chesapeake is at its best in spring and fall, and that is when much of the best cruising is done. Local yacht clubs also support a long season of competition for one-designs and auxiliaries.

One of the pleasantest cruising experiences of all is to know the Chesapeake at its lazy, smiling best in the golden days of October.

The Intracoastal Waterway

Also known informally as the inland waterway, this system of protected creeks, bays, canals, rivers, cuts, sloughs, sounds, inlets, and harbors runs behind the coastline from Maine to Mexico, with a few sections where offshore passage is required; but its heart, the most traveled by cruising boats, runs from Norfolk, Virginia, to Miami, a distance of 1,040 nautical miles.

There is commercial traffic on the ICW and, since most of the waterway must be run under power, it might not seem like the best place for a sailboat cruise. It is really a through highway to the South, but some parts, like the sounds of North Carolina, can provide excellent sailing for a crew that is not on a schedule to push on through. Also, at the speed of an auxiliary sailboat under power, the leisurely pace presents a fine chance to enjoy nature and its varied manifestations of flora and fauna. Forests line much of the waterway, and other parts of the route lie in vast marshes stretching to the horizon and alive with bird life. The ICW may not be a first choice for someone looking for good sailboat cruising, but those who do make use of it can make an extremely enjoyable experience out of the passage.

Florida

The east coast of Florida, with a long, straight coastline backed by the waterway, offers little to the cruising sailor below the St. John's River system near Jacksonville. That broad stream, which flows northward from the jungle-like interior of the state, is wide enough for sailing, but somewhat limited and more suited to powerboats. The Keys, stretching south and west from Miami to Key West along one of the world's great barrier reefs, are the most tropical part of the United States. With water on all sides, and the Gulf Stream swinging by just offshore, they have a warmer climate than the main Florida peninsula, though they can be hit hard by a few northers in winter. The main attraction in the Keys is fishing, and the creeks and channels are a bit confined for good cruising under sail. Miami's Biscayne Bay is excellent for day sailing and weekending as a gateway to the Keys.

The best sailboat cruising in Florida is on the west coast from Tampa Bay southward. Tampa Bay itself has many coves and harbors and a wide expanse of protected water for good sailing, and the area south of it is well supplied with bays, sounds, and inlets. There is good sailing on some of them, but the best cruising drill is to sail in the Gulf of Mexico by day, ducking into one of the many inlets for overnight anchoring. The beaches are white and clean, shell-collecting is a major pastime, and the climate is warm and mild. Drawbacks are lack of wind and an oversupply of thunderstorms in the summer, and a few northers in winter that can really kick up the Gulf. Charter boats are available out of Clearwater and St. Petersburg, and it is a fine area for cruising sailors who want some tropical atmosphere without leaving the country.

The rest of the Gulf of Mexico, curving through Florida's Panhandle, Alabama, Mississippi, and Louisiana to Texas, is not especially hospitable to cruising sailboats, although the Mississippi sounds offer some opportunities for gunkholing. Gulf Coast harbors support local sailing, but there are few visiting cruising yachts.

The Bahamas

A magnet for yachts from all up and down the East Coast, and in fact from all over the world, is the chain of islands lying in the Atlantic off Florida. The Bahamas are actually the tips of land emerging from a 760-mile plateau barely below the surface. The land amounts to about 5,000 square miles in an area of close to 100,000 square miles. The plateau rises steeply for 2,500 feet from the depths of the Atlantic. Its presence off Florida funnels the great natural forces of the

Gulf Stream in a northerly direction, jetting it all the way across to Europe. If the Gulf Stream were not aimed in this way along the eastern coast of North America and on to Europe, these land masses, so important to the history of the civilized world, would be about as livable as Labrador.

The Bahamas are low and scrubby, without pretensions to scenic grandeur. Hills over one hundred feet are rare, and the true beauty lies in the incredible range of water colors that run through every pastel hue of blue and green, backed by the rich blue of the deeps and the whites and tans of the inshore shallows. The warm water is as clear as glass, and bottom details stand out in twenty- and thirty-foot depths.

Nobody knows exactly how many islands there are in this scattered spread. Some of them are mere rocks, and there are also sizable land masses like Andros, Grand Bahamas, Great Abaco, New Providence, Eleuthera, Great Exuma, and Inagua. Some are marshy and impenetrable; others, like Eleuthera, support a good amount of farming. Most of the yachting activity is carried on in the northern half

The Exumas are one of the world's great cruising areas

of the islands, with Nassau, or New Providence—the capital and major port—as the hub. Below Great Exuma, the islands are less developed and less accessible, and only yachtsmen with unlimited time at their command head into the southern islands. Experienced yachtsmen favor the Exumas as one of the great cruising grounds of the world, and the Abacos, with protected water and a wide choice of harbors inside a fringing reef, are the center of bareboat chartering. Both bareboats and professionally crewed charter yachts are available in the Bahamas.

Sailing is great throughout the Bahamas. The prevailing breeze is a southeast trade wind, but the weather is subject to continental influences from North America, modified by the Gulf Stream. In the coldest northers, strong enough to break the warm barrier of air over the Gulf Stream, the temperature can get down into the sixties and, rarely, even a bit colder, but those are odd occasions. Anchorages are limitless in number, varying from modern facilities at luxurious Out Island clubs to isolated gunkholes with not another human in sight. There is no "season" in the Bahamas. The cruising weather is good year-round. Northers do blow in from the continent in winter, and the weather in late summer and early fall may be a bit unsettled, but the constant breezes and great expanses of water keep the temperature at an even level much of the time.

Charts of the Bahamas are not particularly good or reliable, but a commercially published cruising guide, available in most marine supply stores, is detailed, authoritative, and very helpful—in fact indispensable.

In my own cruising, gunkholing the Exumas, with daytime sails across the unbelievable colors and clarity of the waters, and a nighttime anchorage in a secluded creek with not a light or sign of civilization in sight, is one of the supreme cruising experiences. We have returned there many times, and the charm never fades. There are many other great cruising areas, but the Exumas can match any of them.

Caneel Bay, St. John's, a Virgin Islands favorite

The Virgin Islands

Confined in a sixty-mile stretch at the northeast corner of the Caribbean is one of the most compactly perfect cruising areas anywhere, one that has become the world capital for bareboat chartering. In that short string of islands running eastward from St. Thomas in the American Virgins, there are enough anchorages to keep the most dedicated cruising sailor occupied for several weeks. The set-up is therefore ideal for the one- and two-week cruises that are usual in bareboating. Most of the good harbors are in the British half of the Virgins, the eastern section, and Road Town—capital of the BVI, on the island of Tortola—is the busiest charter center anywhere. Several agencies base large fleets of boats here.

The weather varies little year-round in the Virgins, with brisk trades mostly from the easterly quadrant, keeping the temperature equably in the seventies. Winter winds, especially over the Christmas-New

Year's holidays and known as the *Christmas winds,* blow the hardest of all, and late summer can see an easing of the force of the regular trades, with a possibility of an occasional hurricane, about the same percentage as in any other area of the western Atlantic from Martinique to Nova Scotia. Rain usually comes in short squalls that quickly blow by after a fast dousing. A day without sun is a rarity.

Much of the sailing area is protected, though the stronger breezes can kick up a good sea in the more open stretches of Sir Francis Drake Channel, the main waterway at the heart of the Virgins. A good anchorage is never more than an hour away from any spot in the area, so that hard chances are not needed. (The exception is the island of St. Croix, which is off by itself to the south, thirty miles from the other islands and seldom visited by the bareboat fleets.)

Mixed in with the open anchorages in natural surroundings—like the Bight on Norman Island, Trunk Bay, and parts of Gorda Sound—are modern marinas and clubs that cater to cruising yachtsmen with restaurants and docking facilities. Nowhere else in the world has so much cruising packed into such a small area as the Virgin Islands.

The Caribbean

Enjoying the same wind and weather conditions as the Virgins are the rest of the islands of the Caribbean, which string down from Anegada Passage at the eastern end of the Virgins to Grenada, ninety miles from the coast of South America. These are storied islands, rich in history and in local color, each one a small individual world. Just twenty miles away across the heaving blue of a channel can be very different cultures, with English, French, or Dutch antecedents, and the physical features vary, too. Some are mountainous and lush, others lower and more open, such as Antigua, Anguilla, and the Grenadines, but all are scenically gorgeous, and the area is a paradise for the cruising sailor.

Anchored in the incredibly clear waters of the Tobago Cays, highlight of the great cruising in the Grenadines

The most popular cruising area, with a large fleet of bareboats and many professionally crewed charter yachts, is the sixty-mile string of islands known as the Grenadines that lie between St. Vincent and Grenada, divided politically between the two. In my personal ranking, the Grenadines and the Exumas are the two great cruising areas of the Western Hemisphere, adding all characteristics together.

Islands with exotic names like Bequia (pronounced Beck-wee), Mustique, Cannouan, Tobago Cays, Carriacou, and Mayero lie close enough together for easy daytime sailing on a seascape that seems untouched by the rest of the world. There are short open stretches of rough water and some protected sailing in the lee of the islands, touches of civilization in some of the clubs and a boatyard or two, and native life ashore that seems centuries removed. Heart of the Grenadines and most popular of all the harbors is the group known as Tobago Cays—uninhabited, isolated, always breezy, with the clearest, warmest water and most brilliant colors imaginable. All through the Florida Keys, Bahamas, Virgins, and Caribbean, cruising yachtsmen can find excellent snorkeling opportunities, and probably the best of all are here in the Cays, surrounded by a maze of reefs and rocks. I did my first snorkeling here and, unfortunately for subsequent fun, have never seen anywhere else to match it.

North of the Grenadines, the islands are bigger, more mountainous, and more civilized, with shopping and sightseeing taking the place of beachcombing in isolated anchorages. St. Vincent, St. Lucia, Martinique, Dominica, Guadeloupe, and Antigua form a chain plied by professionally crewed charter yachts, with Antigua as a major base. Martinique and Guadeloupe are Departments of France, not colonies, with a colorful life reflecting this fact. Dominica has the poorest harbors and is least developed, with the lushest scenery of all, and each island has its unique attractions. The sailing varies from wet, hard, fast reaches in the open channels between the islands—anywhere from twenty to thirty-five miles across—to idle ghosting in the lee of the high mountains.

The rest of the Caribbean has not been well developed for visiting yachtsmen, and only those with the time to take their own boats on extended cruises have a chance to see such fine cruising areas as the great reef off Belize, the Mexican islands off the Yucatan Peninsula, or Panama's primitive San Blas islands, where the Cuna Indians live as they did in pre-Columbian times. The Venezuelan coast, with its many islands, reminiscent of the Virgins, stringing westward from Isla Margarita to a true atoll known as Los Roques, offers great cruising potential that is only beginning to be realized.

St. George's, Grenada, at the south end of the Lesser Antilles

Inland America

With the development of artificial waterways and lakes for water supply and flood control, vast new areas have opened up in mid-America that can provide cruising areas for sailboats, especially ones that can be trailed behind the family car. Lake systems like the TVA, Kentucky Lake, the Highland Lakes of Texas, Lake Carlisle in Illinois, Lake Champlain, and the Finger Lakes of New York offer wide enough expanses for excellent sailing and facilities, and anchorages that appeal to the cruising sailor.

The Great Lakes

America's great system of inland seas holds a special attraction for cruising sailors, with the only drawback the shortness of the sailing season. Even early June and late September are a bit out of season in parts of the Great Lakes, but midsummer brings out a great fleet of cruising boats. Lake Ontario's best cruising is around the entrance to the St. Lawrence River in the Thousand Islands and the Chaumont-Henderson Harbor area and, on the Canadian side, the graceful Bay of Quinte, extending westward from Kingston. Lake Erie has few cruising opportunities except at its western end, where the islands around Put-in-Bay are an attraction with many good harbors. Lake Huron is the star of the lakes for the cruising sailor, as Georgian Bay and the North Channel on the Canadian side of the lake make up one of the truly classic cruising grounds of the continent. There are uncounted anchorages amid the hundreds of islands, coves, bays, and inlets in an atmosphere of north-country isolation. Rocks and pines line the shores, and the air is crisp and clean. So vast is the spread of undeveloped country that hundreds of boats can operate there with no sense of crowding. Little Current on Manitoulin Island is the hub of this fine cruising ground that extends on to the westward all the way to Sault Sainte Marie and Mackinac Island.

The North Channel of Lake Huron, reminiscent of Maine, and the best Great Lakes cruising area

Lake Superior is the loneliest, most unspoiled, and most challenging of the Great Lakes, little used by yachts because of its remoteness, at least in comparison to the rest of the chain. Its wild, rugged shores are lined with anchorages, and such islands as Isle Royale are a world apart. Weather and sea conditions must be carefully watched.

Lake Michigan's long straight shorelines with widely spaced inlets at cities do not make for relaxed cruising, since there is little protected water, and the runs are fairly long. Not until Green Bay is reached, on the upper western shore, is there a break in the straight beaches; that large indentation provides excellent cruising with many attractive harbors. The Door County peninsula that separates Green Bay from the open lake is a prime target for cruising people.

A drawback to Great Lakes cruising is the unpredictable nature of summer weather, with light breezes prevailing in good weather and the chance of heavy, vicious afternoon thunder-squalls and strong cold fronts as the weather pattern changes. Seas kicked up on the open waters of the Great Lakes can be as dangerous as any on the open ocean and often are steeper and choppier.

Puget Sound

A rich mine of cruising opportunities lies in the Pacific Northwest from Puget Sound on into British Columbia and, for the ruggedly adventurous, all the way to Alaska, but much of the area is more suited to powerboats than cruising auxiliaries because of the strong tidal currents and long periods of light air. To make up for this, there is virtually a year-round season, with mild winter weather, but rain and fog are an expected part of afloat operations in the Northwest. The islands close to Seattle and Tacoma, filling the middle of Puget Sound, make fine weekend targets, and a favorite cruising ground is the San Juan island group that lies between Vancouver Island and the mainland on the United States-Canadian border. Wooded, hilly, and cut through with many protected passages, and popular cruising stops like Orcas Island and Friday Harbor, they enjoy a particularly mild and sunny climate compared to surrounding areas. Beyond them, the Strait of Juan de Fuca leads to wild, rugged, and challenging cruising on the west coast of Vancouver Island amid mountains and unspoiled, forested shores. All through the Puget Sound area, the magnificent snowcapped peaks of mountain ranges on the Olympic Peninsula, and inland to the eastward of the Sound, form the most dramatic backdrop for any cruising ground anywhere, with majestic Mount Rainier as the dominant, most imposing peak of all.

Snow-capped peaks like Mt. Rainier dominate Puget Sound scenery

The San Juan islands attract Pacific Northwest cruising boats

The Pacific Coast

The long unbroken stretch of the West Coast is in dramatic contrast to the East Coast's many indentations and continuous network of protected inland waters. South of Puget Sound there is little opportunity for the cruising sailor except long offshore passages in rough conditions. Oregon's mighty Columbia River supports some local sailing, but it is a difficult area for cruising under canvas, and the next inlet from the Pacific that rates as a yachting center is San Francisco Bay. Here there is great local sailing on virtually a year-round basis, but the only cruising is inland up the Sacramento River Delta, with its twisting sloughs cutting a maze through marshes, fascinating for powerboats but not much for sailing.

Only the Channel Islands off Santa Barbara in southern California offer cruising opportunities under sail, and there are difficulties here. Weather conditions are unpredictable, with heavy incidence of fog, and much of the land area is restricted by the government or private ownership. The rugged, semibarren islands, with steep rocky cliffs and caves lining the shore, and only a few coves for limited anchorage, are dramatically scenic, but the harbors are all exposed to wind shifts, and it is a tricky area for the expert seaman.

Just to the south, Catalina, twenty-five miles offshore from the teeming Los Angeles metropolitan area, has the same sort of scenery and conditions as the Channel Islands. It is the target for weekend cruising by the entire yachting population of the area. The pressures that this imposes on its facilities have meant a form of regimentation unknown in other areas, with fixed moorings in the coves controlled by various clubs and organizations. The casual visitor doesn't just drop in and drop anchor on a normally busy weekend. Moorings must be reserved in advance, a system that also applies in the string of artificial harbors that supports yachting throughout the region.

Catalina's coves all provide protection from one direction only. Those on the seaward side are open to the prevailing westerlies, so that the north shore, facing the mainland, usually is the protected side. Havoc can be wrought here, however, when a sudden santana, a hot desert northeaster blowing off the land with great force, turns this side of the island into a dangerous lee shore. Experienced Catalina visitors are ever on the alert for this phenomenon, which often comes with little warning. The other problem of the area is fog, a fairly steady companion to boating operations.

A Cal 2-46 in a cove on Catalina in off-season; all buoys would be occupied on a normal weekend

San Diego, at the Mexican border, has a year-round climate that permits continuous activity afloat, and it is also the gateway to the most popular cruising on the West Coast. Short junkets to ports like Ensenada or the Coronado Islands just south of San Diego are good for weekending or a week, but the major cruising thrust is to the long finger of Baja California and the Gulf of California that lies inside it. This is a major project requiring weeks or months in a sailboat, and Californians often do it in stages, changing crews at various ports and commuting to their boats. The seacoast of Baja is a long, arid stretch with a few fascinating stops, and it is a long slug to windward to return northward along it. The Gulf, however, with its brilliant clear waters, starkly dramatic desert scenery, isolated fishing villages, and hundreds of deserted islands and coves, is a major cruising ground. La Paz is the major resort and yachting center. Mexican regulations are complex and tricky, never predictable, and local officials are often difficult, but Baja is its own reward.

Because of the great distances between cruising areas on the Pacific Coast, and the lure of the distant islands of the Pacific, there is a much greater tradition of offshore cruising than on the Atlantic Coast. Where a New Englander is content with Maine's myriad coves and bracing air or the salty charms of Nantucket or the Vineyard, and even the Bahamas and Caribbean are relatively close, the Pacific-cruising sailor has far wider horizons, thinking in terms of the Hawaiian Islands 2,300 miles away, or the Marquesas, Tuamotus, and Society Islands, more than twice that distance away in the South Pacific. The numbers are small in comparison to the boats crowding Cuttyhunk or Catalina on a Saturday night, but there is an ever-growing fleet of adventurers that thinks in terms of these distant targets where cruising under sail is concerned.

___16

The Long Voyagers

TO THE majority of sailors, cruising means daytime passages between interesting harbors, with a pleasant night at anchor or plugged in to the amenities of a marina, and perhaps an occasional overnight run. To a special breed, however, it is the challenge of the open sea and of lonely distances between continents. Cape Horn, the Tuamotus, Torres Strait, the Seychelles, and Durban are the sort of names dropped in that set, and its members think in increments of 3,600-mile passages instead of a 36-mile run to the next harbor.

They are alike in their freedom from the ordinary pleasures and restraints of civilization, but they differ greatly among themselves. Some sail only to get to exotic ports. They endure a multiweek stint at sea for the rewards of Papeete or Cocos Keeling. Others are happy only in the solitude of the sea, far from land, in the tiny world of a small sailboat. Some sail with spouses or companions; others prefer to be alone and on their own. In common they have courage, stamina, patience, self-sufficiency, and the need to dance to a different tune from the rest of the human race. Some psychologists have called it a form of suicide; others think of it as a less radical, more subdued rejection of social values and ordinary human relationships. Almost everyone who has never done it looks on those who do as at least a little bit crazy, and the fact that there are more and more people out there every day, sailing the lonely sea paths in small sailboats, may be some form of commentary on the current state of civilization.

Joshua Slocum, as we have seen, is their patron saint. There were small-boat voyagers before him, and not just the Captain Blighs forced into fantastic feats of small-boat seamanship by a turn of fate. Professional seamen ventured across oceans in small boats looking for publicity and profits, just as some do today, but Slocum was the first to become a public figure. When he returned in 1898 at age fifty-four from his circumnavigation in the clumsy thirty-six-foot *Spray,* a rebuilt derelict oyster boat rescued from a pasture in Fair Haven, Massachusetts, he was a celebrity of the first rank, and the world marveled at his story.

Captain Joshua Slocum in "Spray" showed the way to long voyagers

It was a good, salty one, and he told it well in his book *Sailing Alone Around the World.* Anecdotes of the trip, such as that about the spreading of carpet tacks on his deck while at anchor in Tierra del Fuego so that any savages who might try to sneak aboard during the night would give themselves away with their surprised cries, became widely known. (No one ever bothered to ask why carpet tacks happened to be on a small sailboat.) He was a fine seaman and a colorful character, though his personal life was not happy. It is one of the eternal mysteries of the sea that he was lost with *Spray* without a trace, on a voyage to South America in 1910.

Slocum's immediate successors were commercially inspired to try to cash in on his fame. Captain John Voss from Vancouver, British Columbia, managed to get around the world in a thirty-seven-foot dugout canoe, rigged as a three-masted schooner, which he obtained from an Indian for a good price by getting the Indian drunk. Called *Tilikum,* she was an even more unlikely vessel for the purpose than the boxy *Spray,* but Voss finally made it after a series of adventures and misadventures. He did not do it solo, as various crew members were with him for part of the voyage.

Thomas Fleming Day, editor of *Rudder* magazine, to demonstrate the feasibility of long small-boat voyages, sailed a small, hard-chine yawl of his own design, named *Seabird,* across to the Mediterranean in 1911, developing considerable publicity in the process. He had also been instrumental in getting the Bermuda Race started. The race, as we have seen, and long-distance sailboat passages, gave way to World War I, but the new freedoms of the 1920s sent a larger group of sailors off on long voyages, though it was still a rare feat for a small sailboat to cross an ocean or circle the globe, and it was automatically good for a book if the sailor survived and could spell his own name.

One of the better-known adventurers of the twenties and thirties was Harry Pidgeon, an Iowa farm boy who built *Islander,* a Seabird yawl like Day's, for one thousand dollars and went around the world twice, taking plenty of time to make new friends in the ports he visited.

Alain Gerbault, a French tennis champion who turned into a deep-sea voyager, was one of the champion loners of all, disappearing for years at a time in the South Pacific. His vessel was the highly unsuitable deep, narrow cutter *Firecrest,* so slow and decrepit that his passages were tortuously long.

William Albert Robinson (no relation to this author) made a world circumnavigation in the thirty-two-foot ketch *Svaap* that was closely followed through his articles and books. One of the best writers to make a long passage was Richard Maury, who sailed the little Nova Scotia schooner *Cimba* to the Fiji Islands, where the voyage ended in the loss, to him, of the boat on a reef at the entrance to Suva Harbor, though it was later salvaged and recommissioned locally.

In another type of operation, Irving Johnson and Exy Johnson, his wife, began a series of circumnavigations, taking eighteen months to the day, in a pilot schooner they named *Yankee.* For crew they had young men and women who were willing to pay for the privilege of working the vessel. They got their money's worth in adventure, seamanship experience, and visits to remote, exotic, and exciting areas. The voyages were models of planning and execution and were taken up again after World War II, in which Johnson's familiarity with unusual areas was put to use in survey work. A larger brigantine, also named *Yankee,* continued in the fine traditions the Johnsons had established, operating until 1958. After that they turned to a smaller ketch, in which they ranged the rivers and waterways of Europe with small charter parties for more than fifteen years in a continued example of the highest standards of adventurous seamanship.

The proliferation of voyages between the two world wars was as nothing compared to the tremendous increase in activity after World War II. Every voyager used to make news, but there has to be something very unusual about the boat or skipper nowadays to attract special attention, for hundreds of boats are continually swarming across the sea lanes. The run from Europe to the Caribbean via the Azores, Canaries, Cape Verdes, or Madeira to one of the islands in the Lesser Antilles is the most traveled, but the Pacific is also dotted with yachts seeking far horizons. A visitor to the remote, colorful Marquesas, returning in 1975 after an absence of several years, was amazed to find half a dozen yachts in anchorages that had seemed like undiscovered paradises on the previous visit. The Marquesas are over four thousand miles from mainland yachting centers, not just over the horizon like the Bahamas or West Indies.

In the fall, a flood of yachts heads from the northeastern United States to the Caribbean. Most of them take the coastal route to Morehead City, North Carolina, in October and head offshore from there in the period between late-summer hurricanes and winter storms.

Others try the offshore route across the Gulf Stream to Bermuda, taking a break there before heading south, but this method is fraught with uncertainties and has brought trouble to many who have tried it. This, incidentally, has nothing to do with the so-called Bermuda Triangle, which is a figment of the imagination of sensationalist magazine and book authors. The same forces that are at work at sea anywhere in the world also apply in this area, which supposedly has Bermuda at the apex, and Miami and Puerto Rico at the bottom corners, of the triangle. Storms, collisions with freighters or tankers at night or in rough weather, structural failures, human errors, and encounters with whales can sink vessels any time they venture offshore, and all the so-called mysteries of the Triangle have been shown to have perfectly logical explanations when sufficiently researched. The book *The Bermuda Triangle Mystery — Solved* by Lawrence Kusche did a particularly fine job in debunking the ghost stories of some of the sensationalists.

The Triangle area is sufficiently challenging in its natural conditions without the addition of any occult forces, and boats taking the offshore route in the fall almost always encounter severe gales. It is not the recommended route for anything but large, well-found, and well-staffed yachts.

Out of all that voyaging, one might expect that some doctrine has been developed on the best type of boat for the purpose, but the boats used for long voyaging have been as diverse as the people who sail them. One reason is that many of the long voyagers are shoestring operators and are forced to make do with whatever they can manage within their budget. We have discussed cruising boat types in Chapter 13, and the subject of multihulls always comes up, especially with budget-minded sailors. Despite the success of many multihull voyages and the advantages of initial stability, low cost, and speed on some points of sailing, most experienced sailors do not approve of them for offshore passaging. Construction weaknesses and the impossibility of righting one after a capsize are the main reasons.

Probably the basics for a good offshore boat can be boiled down to a few generalities. It must naturally be strongly built in hull and rig, and the lines should be seakindly, which means fairly heavy displacement. A light boat that fights waves rather than accommodating them is corky, quick, and uncomfortable in a seaway. A long keel and good-sized rudder make for good steering characteristics. Some people think double-enders take following seas best, but not all do. The rig should be easily managed and compact, and some form of twin staysails or boomed jibs is almost mandatory for long passages. There should be plenty of stowage space for food, water, equipment, and spare parts, since the long-voyaging boat should be virtually self-sufficient.

Most important of all is self-steering. Especially if a boat is single-handed or has a small crew, long hours spent in helm duty can be debilitating and just plain boring, and there is little chance to do other ship's work. Good self-steering mechanisms are available, and they should be of first priority for the long voyager. The basic principle, though the mechanics can vary, is to have a vane activated by the wind that is attached to the rudder and counteracts the tendency of the wind on the sails to affect the rudder. The force of the sails tends to make the boat go one way, but the wind on the vane will

A Chinese lugsail rig and self-steerer for ease of single-handling

counteract this and keep the boat on a desired course. There are tremendous strains on self-steering mechanisms, and they must be very strongly geared and well engineered. Only a tiny minority of long voyagers get along without them.

The paperwork of long voyaging bothers some people, and red tape can be difficult in strange ports. Every country has its peculiarities, and one of the most popular forms of make-work throughout the world is to create a job for someone to bang a rubber stamp on documents. Ship's papers should be in order, and some owners have learned the trick of having a document gotten up—covered with ribbons, seals, stamps, and official script—that proclaims the vessel to be a vessel, or some such startling statement. That and the greased palm are two of the most effective means of cutting red tape, but, seriously, it is vital to check ahead with the consulate of a country to be visited concerning the requirements of entry there. Often, advance notice can reduce the chances for misunderstanding and resultant difficulties.

Although careful advance planning on the boat and on handling red tape is recommended, many a voyager picks up stakes in the most casual way and still manages to wander safely into Grenada or Honolulu at the end of a long passage. Home-built boxes with venetian blinds for sails (well, that's what they look like) have made it to the West Indies from Europe, and it would probably not cause much surprise in Barbados or Grenada to see a bale of hay come floating in from Gibraltar via the Canaries with a parasol as a sail.

As mentioned, it is only the unusual voyages that manage to get attention nowadays, so routine are the passages on the well-traveled routes by conventionally well-found, well-sailed yachts. A feat like that of young Robin Graham—who sailed the twenty-four-foot sloop *Dove* around the world, starting out at the age of sixteen as the youngest circumnavigator and ending up with a wife and a new, bigger boat (and a yen to retire to a ranch)—attracts great attention through magazine sponsorship, books, and an eventual movie, but for every Robin Graham there are hundreds of young drifters sailing around in anonymous obscurity.

Robert Manry, a copy desk editor on a Cleveland newspaper, broke the bonds of that routine existence by fulfilling a lifelong dream: sailing the thirteen-foot sloop *Tinkerbelle* across the Atlantic. The project started modestly in obscurity but attracted the attention of copy desk men the world over and was blown into a major event. His record of being the smallest was broken by an airline pilot named Hugo Vihlen, who managed the improbable feat of sailing a six-foot boat from Africa to Florida. The smallest boat to sail around the world was John Guzzwell's twenty-foot yawl *Trekka,* in a fine feat of seamanship in the late fifties. Guzzwell has continued to sail, living with his wife and sons aboard his handsome home-built forty-five-foot sloop *Treasure.* Anne Davidson was the first woman to cross the Atlantic single-handed, sailing the twenty-three-foot sloop *Felicity Ann* over in 1953, but a few female sailors have emulated her. Many husband-and-wife teams have made long and unusual

John Guzzwell, in his home-built "Treasure," is one of the world's most accomplished long voyagers

voyages, however. Circumnavigations by Sten and Brita Holmdahl of Sweden, and Bill and Phyllis Crow of Honolulu, in the fifties, set examples; the Trinidad couple of Harold and Kwailan LaBorde—with their young sons with them for most of the passage—went around in their home-built ketch *Hummingbird* in the sixties. They caused some consternation in South Pacific islands where the natives had never seen anyone but whites in yachts, and they also had apartheid difficulties in South Africa, which were fortunately surmounted by the individual friendship of local yachtsmen. Britishers Susan and Eric Hiscock have been among the most persistent, and literate, voyagers of all, continually on the move, and Hal and Margaret Roth circumnavigated the Pacific and South America in the thirty-five-foot sloop *Whisper* and made significant contributions to yachting literature in the process in the sixties and seventies.

There have been special races and stunt events fostered by the long-voyaging vogue, usually under British sponsorship, with

Sir Francis Chichester dramatized
single-handling as few others have

Chichester's "Gipsy Moth" with visitors aboard in Sydney, Australia

commercial considerations paramount. Sir Francis Chichester became one of the better-known adventurers of the twentieth century through his victories in single-handed transatlantic races and his highly publicized circumnavigation on *Gipsy Moth*. A single-handed around-the-world race in the late sixties was won by Robin Knox-Johnston almost by default. Many entrants ran into difficulties, and one, Donald Crowhurst, evidently committed suicide off his trimaran *Teignmouth Electron* after sending false messages about his progress around the world while in reality remaining in the Atlantic until a suitable time for heading back to the finish. The eccentric French voyager Bernard Moitessier started in the race and went on around the Cape of Good Hope and the Horn, but then, instead of heading north to the finish in England, decided to continue on around Africa and Australia again to end up in Tahiti. His reason was that he just couldn't face the civilized world again.

For every one of these unusual individuals, several hundred boats are wending their way along the sea lanes at this very moment, and being joined by more every year, with families aboard and parents conducting correspondence course school for the children, or with married couples or groups of friends quietly pursuing a way of life that has changed from the freak category into a very real factor in the sailing world.

___17

ℱ Summing Up

VERY OFTEN I am asked, "What is your favorite cruising ground?" or "What kind of sailing do you like best?" Questions are posed about my ideal boat, the kind of racing I prefer, and what my most exciting experiences have been. "How did you manage to keep sailing when your children were little?" is another rather plaintive query from young marrieds.

The answers can never be pat and easy. Most "bests" and "ideals" have to be qualified, and personal solutions for our family might not work as well for others. The rewards of sailing are so personal, so subjective, and so dependent on individual likes and needs that everybody's answers are different. In looking back, though, over my own experiences since I first held a tiller in my hand in the summer of 1926 at Nantucket, Massachusetts, there are, of course, certain experiences and memories that do stand out from the others as symbols of what sailing has meant to me personally. Since I have managed to tie in my career with sailing since 1947, I have naturally had a great many extra opportunities to enjoy it and have been able to taste more varied joys and delights.

Although I was taken sailing when I was seven in 1926 and was at least aware of what it was like to be under sail in a boat, and saw a great amount of sailboat racing while lending what must have been rather dubious assistance on the committee boat to my uncle, who was Fleet Captain of Nantucket YC, I didn't become really involved until 1931 while at Camp Viking on Cape Cod's Pleasant Bay. That was a sailing camp, and we really did learn to sail. The camp boats were simply rigged little sharpies, actually flat-bottomed centerboard rowboats with one low-aspect Marconi sail, and a couple of Baybirds, fifteen-foot round-bilge, gaff-rigged sloops that were a local one-design class.

The chance to sail every day was very exciting, and I remember well the day when everything fell together and it suddenly came to me that I knew how to sail. The whole camp was going on a special picnic to an island in the bay, and some of us who had seemed to grasp what it was about were put in the sharpies for a "distance race" of what was probably two or three miles. There was a good sou'wester blowing, making the course to the island a beat, and during it we worked out a tremendous lead over the other boats. At the tiller, I suddenly became really aware, for the first time, of lifts and headers and how they affected the boat, and we played them well, tacking on headers several times. A great feeling of the power I possessed in controlling the boat and getting the most out of her surged through me. I had never been much of an athlete in the usual land sports, and here, for the first time, I was a winner in a very concrete way. It was great to look back at the other boats and see our lead over them increase as we reacted to lifts and puffs. I wish I could remember the name of my crew, but I do remember the wonderful feeling of teamwork as we hiked out and kept the boat flat when the puffs hit, and the sense of control I felt in handling the tiller.

The confidence I gained in that one sail made a tremendous difference to a twelve-year-old who had never been very sure of himself. It was something I had done on my own. The decisions had been mine, and the feel of the boat reacting to my hand on the tiller, as I reacted to the wind, was a new and wonderful sensation. From then on I nourished the feeling deep inside me, and it nourished me and gave me confidence not only in sailing, but also in everything else I did. Buoyed by the excitement of winning that race, I went on to win the camp championship regatta in Baybirds at the end of the summer and receive the sailing medal. At that awkward age, the edge of adolescence, I had found something special that was for me, and I can't think of any one experience that has helped me more as an enrichment of life. I even played baseball, football, and tennis with more aplomb, if not more skill, and, as an individual, I had an inner security that made me feel like much more of a person. That special feeling about sailing has never left me. Sailing may not be looked on often as therapy for insecure adolescents or as an ingredient in a Dale Carnegie course, but it was truly a turning point for me, and a life determinant, to "discover" it that day on Pleasant Bay.

There could be a string of "I remembers" almost as long as the rest of this book if I were to catalogue every fine moment enjoyed in a sailboat, but there are some special highlights that bear touching on, and some answers to those questions that are popped at me so frequently.

As for preferences, the one on cruising grounds is the toughest to narrow down. I have often said that, given the chance for just one more cruise, it would be a tough choice between the Exumas and the Grenadines, but that leaves out such areas as southern New England, Maine, the Aegean, the Chesapeake, and many others. In season and given a break in the weather, all of them are great, but, with the thumbscrews twisting tighter, I guess my forced answer would be for the Grenadines, although I would call the Pipe Creek area in the central Exumas about as delightful a cruising target as I could imagine.

As for the ideal boat, there is no such thing. Every boat is a compromise, as we have seen time and again in the descriptions and analyses in this book. We have partially solved the problem in our

Great anchorages, like this cove in Maine's Somes Sound, are part of many "I remembers"

family by having one boat for day sailing and one-design racing at home, and another for longer-range cruising. For our circumstances, the eighteen-foot Sanderling Class catboat *is* ideal for home use on the Jersey Coast's Shrewsbury River. She is a fiberglass replica of the classic Cape Cod cat, a beamy, shallow-draft, gaff-rigged centerboarder that sails very well, is roomy and comfortable for day-sailing parties, and provides close and exciting racing, one-design in every respect, in a fleet of more than twenty boats at our local Shrewsbury Sailing and YC. She is no racing machine, but the competition is so even, with strict one-design provisions and many good sailors in the fleet, that it is very exciting and rewarding. Also, the boat does not require intensive maintenance and elaborate tuning between races. Some enjoy that aspect of racing. I don't have the time or the inclination.

Our cruising boat for nine years was a twenty-four-foot light-displacement sloop, one of the Controversy types developed in Maine by boat builder Farnham Butler. The smallest of the Controversies, she was called the Amphibi-Ette, since she was built to be trailed, and we took advantage of this feature many times. She was trailed to Maine, the southern New England area, Florida, and the Great Lakes and was also shipped by steamship to the Bahamas on her trailer. She suited us perfectly when our three children were teenagers, and we had many great family cruises in her. She also was fast enough to race successfully in handicap events. She eventually became a sacrifice to tuition bills, but, finally finished in that league, we are back as cruising-boat owners with a Morgan Out Island 36 sloop—a center-cockpit, aft-cabin model that adapts well to our station in life. She is small enough for us to handle easily as a couple, without crew problems, and big enough to be very comfortable for four while cruising. With the separate cabins and a head and shower in each, the privacy is perfect, an important factor, and there is more room when needed for invasions by our offspring and the grandchildren. She sails well, has a good turn of speed (7.5 knots) under power with a 40-horsepower diesel, and has a moderate draft of 3-foot-9 for cruising flexibility. The center cockpit and after cabin give her a chunky look that is not quite clipper-like, but beauty has always been an adjunct of function (within reasonable limits), as far as I'm concerned. In that inevitable compromise, mentioned so often, the sleek lines of a miniaturized great yacht often mean cramped discomfort and limited use of space in boats under forty feet.

I'm not saying that the catboat, *Polly,* or the OI 36, *Tanagra,* are ideal boats for everyone. They just happen to suit us well at the moment.

As for racing, I prefer one-design competition to handicap racing. Some of the most exciting sails I've ever experienced have been in distance races, and the Amphibi-Ette, *Mar Claro,* won her share of prizes. She was always well down the scratch list, however, as one of the smallest boats, and in some of the races we won, the larger boats we had beaten on time allowance would already be in the harbor with sails furled and the crews no longer sober in the bar by the time we finished. I found this less esthetically pleasing than the sensation of getting the gun as you cross the line and looking over the stern at all the competition behind you. That experience in the sharpie at Camp Viking must have had a long-lasting effect in many ways.

Also, ever since Navy days in World War II when, as skipper of a 110-foot subchaser, I had to take her out on orders no matter what the weather or circumstances, I have looked upon going to sea on schedule, despite the weather, as more work than pleasure. That has colored my attitude toward ocean racing as much as the artistic objection to winning on paper rather than boat-for-boat. These are purely personal observations of choice, which is why I own a one-design and a cruising boat, leaving the ocean racers to those who find them fascinating, but some of my most exciting moments afloat have been in ocean racers.

Probably the most memorable was the 1960 Bermuda Race as crew aboard the seventy-one-foot ketch *Barlovento.* That was the race that was dusted by the heaviest blow in the history of the event, an unpredicted and fast-moving disturbance, just short of hurricane strength, the night before arrival in Bermuda. *Barlovento,* a husky, steel Phil Rhodes-designed ketch that is more of a cruising yacht than an ocean racer, went through the blow under full main and staysail, passing half the fleet. Rail-down, with the leech of her mainsail vibrating like a manic machine-gun, she charged through the noisy night in an incredible display of power under sail. Squalls within the larger storm brought sudden changes in wind strength and direction, and one of the wildest came when I was at the wheel. We tacked in what seemed like a header and then could not fill away on the other tack for 180°, as the wind swung wildly around and rain burst across us in slashing sheets. It was truly a night to remember, and the knowledge, next morning, of having survived it, as the sun burned through departing clouds and the sea turned from menacing black to a bright, shining blue, was especially satisfying.

The other ocean racing experience that stands out above many others came in the 1969 Miami-Nassau Race. I had been lent an Irwin 31 sloop, and we were the smallest boat on the scratch list of 105 entries. The first part of the race was a fast reach across the Gulf Stream in a strong southerly. As we passed Great Isaac Light, the gateway to the Bahamas at the entrance to Northwest Providence Channel, and squared away down the channel, reaching at hull speed in a welter of foam, a build-up of clouds in the northwest told us that a weather change was coming. Lightning played in among the towers of thunderheads, while the local clouds, racing in from the southwest as the wind continued to veer and send us rapidly on the way, scudded across a late moon. Patches of brightness plated the water briefly as the moon peeked through.

The front heralded by the thunderheads caught us at the end of the midwatch. Lightning zipped between the clouds and thunder crashed directly overhead, while sheets of cold rain swallowed us in their pelting embrace and the wind switched crazily from one point to another. When the heaviest rain had passed, the wind settled into the northwest and began to blow even harder than the southerly had, and dawn found us passing Stirrup Cay, the turning point for the last leg down to Nassau, with the wind piping up over forty knots and mountainous seas building on our stern. They loomed up like deep blue Alps, crested with the snow of breaking whitecaps, and each one looked as though it would crash down and engulf the little sloop. Time and again, however, her stern lifted to the onrushing seas, and with the helmsman of the moment concentrating mightily on avoiding a broach, she would rise to each sea, surf on it for a quick, exhilarating moment, drop in the trough, and rise again to meet the next one. With a deep-reefed mainsail and the smallest Genoa wung out on the spinnaker pole, the boat had all the sail she could handle, and there was no way a boat of that size could go any faster. There were tentative discussions about using a storm spinnaker, until we saw a few boats around us try theirs with immediate, disastrous results. Seeing their chutes break loose and stream off to leeward out of control after a couple of wild broaches by the boat, we decided that discretion was not chicken and remained with the combination we had.

It was one of the wildest sleighrides I've ever experienced, and we surfed into the entrance to Nassau harbor—thankful that it had been made a deep-water port and was no longer subject to "rages" on the bar—in early afternoon, making the 184-mile passage from Miami in the incredible time of twenty-six hours. *Windward Passage*, the seventy-three-foot maxi ketch that later set the Transpac record, broke the course record in the amazing time of 15:54:17. She had passed us soon after the start (big boats went off last), making an impressive twelve knots in a stirring spectacle, but such are the vagaries of handicapping that the race was a shoo-in for small boats. Our class took the

A great boat for our home waters, the Sanderling catboat: after the race, a quiet sail home, and everything's right with the world

first three fleet prizes. We were fifth in class and fifteenth in fleet; *Passage,* which had charged ahead about as fast as a sailboat could be expected to go, ended up fifty-fifth in fleet on corrected time. It was a great experience but the results illustrate why I like one-design racing better as far as the satisfactions of competition go. But I will never forget that sail and the look of the big blue seas looming up astern, lifting the boat and sending her on a wild surfing surge with wings of water shooting out on each side halfway up to the spreaders. When fast sailing is tinged with dread, the exhilaration is all the stronger.

Cruising, though, has brought the greatest rewards. The only competition is the forces of nature, but there is a great satisfaction in having conquered them and completed a passage. It need not be rough or dramatic, and some of the most satisfying ones have been peacefully serene. Cruising has taken us to many exotic areas of the globe, and experiencing them from the deck of a sailboat that we are operating ourselves adds an extra measure of fulfillment.

The first foreign landfall in my own boat was a special moment. It was in *Mar Claro.* We had trailed her to Florida for the winter, and Christmas vacation was spent exploring the Florida Keys with the whole family aboard, a thoroughly successful operation. In the spring, we came back to her without the children and, almost on the spur of the moment, took off from Key Largo for the Bahamas, encouraged by ideal weather. The fresh southerly that had promised a fast reach across died when we were halfway there, and we did some slow drifting and even a bit of powering, finally picking up the lights of Bimini, on the edge of the Gulf Stream, an hour or so after midnight. Under a late moon, we swept toward the low line of the island, reaching across a freshening breeze over water silvered by the slanting moonpath, the bow wave curling away rhythmically and the wake gleaming whitely astern. Suddenly the darkness of deep water gave way to a ghostly white as we came onto the bar at the entrance to Bimini, the bottom details standing in sharp relief in the clear, moonlit water. When we eased into the harbor and found a berth at a pier, the warm wind that rustled the palm fronds along the shore washed over us with a scent of tide-bared sand flats, wood smoke, and flowers. It was a tremendously satisfying moment.

Cruising has brought many more of them, some of spray-splashed excitement, others of peace and serenity. There has never been a better night at anchor than in Warderick Wells in the Exumas, with a cloudless sky, brimming with stars, and not a light to be seen in any direction, alone in a deep blue pool protected by a white expanse of flats. The Bahamas have provided many of the best cruising memories: nine days of reaching breezes and clear skies in April while *Mar Claro* ranged the Exumas; a swift run from Eleuthera across the deep blue of Exuma Sound in *Tanagra*, averaging over seven knots on a passage to Highborne Cay, sweeping in between wave-dashed rocks to the serenity of the anchorage; a night at anchor on the Great Bahamas Bank between Cat Cay and Chub Cay, with the water so calm and the vessel so motionless that it was the only time in my life I have ever experienced absolute, total silence, the complete absence of sound of any kind; a leisurely glide through Pipe Creek and its incredible range of water colors from deep, inky blue to the palest pastels of green and oyster white in the shallows.

In other waters there was the unmatched blue of the Aegean against an arid backdrop of islands dotted by wind-twisted, lonely trees on the hillsides and the dusty green of olive groves. Nowhere else is there a wind like the *meltemi*, the clear-weather phenomenon that blasts southward across the central Aegean at over forty knots under warm, smiling skies. With the right sail combination—deep-reefed and a small staysail—a smashing, crashing reach across a *meltemi* is one of the rare experiences in cruising.

The interisland passages in the Lesser Antilles where the trades blow unhindered all the way from Africa, building up a mightly roll of sea, are the same kind of sailing—fast, wet, exciting, and better when they are over than when the spray is flying, but never forgotten afterward. A constant fascination is the play of colors on the islands ahead and astern. The deep green of the vegetation of the island close astern gradually fades to a misty purple, while the island ahead goes through a reverse transformation. In the Grenadines, the islands are lower, browner, and more wind-swept, and the sailing is great. A night at anchor in the Tobago Cays after a brisk sail to get there, with the wind humming through the rigging, and the chuckle and lap-lap of water along the hull as added accompaniment, is one of the great experiences in cruising, even with the increased influx of charter yachts. When we first went there in 1962, we were alone in the anchorage, and after the sunset glow faded over Mayero on the western horizon, there was not a light to be seen in the entire circumference of the horizon, while the Southern Cross and Polaris opposed each other to starboard and port.

Nearer home, there have been quiet sails on Chesapeake Bay on golden October afternoons, swift runs up Buzzards Bay and Vineyard Sound before the smoky sou'westers of August, and the crisp, clean, pine-scented air of a Maine harbor in the morning. Much of our cruising in these waters was with our children as they were growing up, the culmination of years of sailing with them from their first months onward. There is no better way, to my mind, to get to know your children than to sail with them, and it has been one of the major influences in our family life. We have seen the timidity of young parents who stay away from sailing because they feel their children are too young, which has always seemed a sad mistake. When they are little, the routine should be adjusted to their level, without pressure and without forcing the issue. If it is relaxed fun, they thrive on sailing, but short attention-spans should be catered to. All three of ours have remained ardent sailors into adulthood and have made it an important part of their own lives.

Different from the joys of cruising and the adventures in distant waters that cruising has led us to is the fun of one-design racing, which has been a big part of our life at home. Each child was given a boat at age nine. Two took to it right away and kept it up all through adolesence. The third was not competitive as a teenager and dropped out of racing by choice for several years, though continuing to enjoy sailing as a social pleasure, especially cruising. Later, she became very competitive as a young adult.

With the children grown up and moved away, and the Comets, Turnabouts, Wood Pussies, Blue Jays, and 420s no longer a part of our sailing life, the catboat has taken over as the family racing machine, focus of weekend involvement. There have been victories and, more often, there have been defeats, but sailboat racing is such a challenge that a seventh place can sometimes be almost as exciting as getting the gun if you have managed to outtack a long-time rival on the last beat to the finish, or pulled a neat inside overlap on a couple of boats at the leeward mark. There is nothing quite like the sound of the gun, though, at the end of a tense race, and the memory of a close finish that went your way as you hiked out, kept her flat, and squeezed up to the line on that last favorable puff is enough to keep you coming back through many an also-ran finish, working to get there again at the head of the fleet.

That is a short version of what sailing has meant to me, a capsule of almost endless pleasures and rewards. Through it all, one image recurs as central, the most typical example of the joy I find in being a sailor. It is nothing dramatic or exotic. I am not making a dawn landfall on Rarotonga or rounding the Horn in a gale. I am not winning the SORC, and I am not even making an afternoon anchorage in the Bahamas, Buzzards Bay, or the Chesapeake after a fine day's sail. These are images I enjoy, and the ones I have actually experienced have been tremendously exciting and enriching, but the basic one, the ultimate symbol of everyday satisfaction, is closer to home.

It is late afternoon, and we have finished a couple of hard races at the club. Perhaps I have won at least one of them, and that of course makes it better, but even without a win, it has been fun to compete, to go all-out for a while in intense concentration, husband and wife working together as a team, knowing each other well in what we both contribute to the race. We have had a beer and a postrace rehash at the club float, and now it is time to head for home, two miles away. The sea breeze that has given us fine racing conditions is beginning to ease off now, the sun is lowering inland, and its slanting light bathes the far shore in a golden glow. Sedge banks and sand dunes gleam in the mellow chiaroscuro as we cast off and reach across the light chop left over from the stronger breeze. Sunpath dances over the water astern, seagulls fly high overhead on their way in from the ocean to a night's resting place in the marshes, and the water is darker and bluer. Cold drink in hand, I steer casually, a foot against the tiller, in contrast to the concentration of the race as we glide slowly homeward, perhaps talking a bit about the details of the race, perhaps silently enjoying the approach of evening. The knowledge is deep within me that there is really no place else I would want to be at this moment. This is where I belong, everything is right, and I am happy to be here. That's sailing.

Index